FROM FLYING BOATS TO FLYING JETS

David,

Hope you enjoy reading
of the other "me"

Eric Woods

10 — 12 — 02

FROM FLYING BOATS TO FLYING JETS

Flying in the Formative Years of BOAC
1946 - 1972

ERIC (TIMBER) WOODS

Airlife
England

Copyright © Eric Woods 1997

First Published in 1997 by
Airlife Publishing Ltd.

British Library Cataloguing-in-Publication Data

A catalogue record for this book is
available from the British Library

ISBN 1 85310 837 5

Typeset by Hewer Text Composition Services, Edinburgh
Printed in England by St Edmundsbury Press Ltd, Bury St Edmunds,
Suffolk

Airlife Publishing Ltd
101 Longden Road, Shrewsbury SY2 9EB, England.

CONTENTS

FOREWORD

Although the British Overseas Airways Corporation operated a variety of limited services during the period 1939/1946, it was not until hostilities had finally ceased, that the Corporation really geared up for the rapid expansion in passenger, freight and mail services which were to follow.

After demobilisation from the Royal Air Force, the author had, what he considers to be, the good fortune on joining BOAC, to be moved to the unit which operated the civil version of the giant Short Bros Sunderland flying boats out of Poole and Southampton, as they rapidly reopened the pre-war Imperial Airways routes to the Near and Far East and South Africa.

To say that these services were like no others, is an understatement, made clear as the very nature of flying boat operations, seen through the eyes of an aircraft navigator, unfolds in this story.

Sadly, for sound economical reasons, flying boat operations ceased, and the author moved to other fields.

He goes on to relate the build up of replacement flights by the Argonaut type aeroplane, followed by the massive training programme set up to prepare *ab initio*, and ex-service pilots, for their future roles as civilian captains and co-pilots.

The story continues by covering further aircraft replacement programmes, as larger and more powerful machines came along and routes were extended, culminating, finally, in a worldwide network.

Coupled with this, the author also highlights the expansion of the training system whereby pilots were somewhat reluctantly obliged to add navigational qualifications to their civil licences, to cover the pending departure of full-time navigators, as company policy.

Technical data has been kept to a minimum, and the picture has been built up by the use of anecdotes, both amusing and serious.

This book should appeal to all civilian flight crew members, whether they were directly involved or not, and will certainly open up a new world to those who would dearly love to fly, but cannot participate for one reason or another.

INTRODUCTION

Having had a book of wartime flying memoirs published in the recent past, I was pleasantly surprised at the number of complimentary and unsolicited responses.

There is obviously an interested public out there, just as there are many experienced aviators with a story to tell, although the latter are disinclined to put pen to paper.

With this in mind, it seemed that a natural follow up to my wartime autobiography would be to record the twenty years following my departure from the Royal Air Force, and during which I flew on worldwide routes with our National Airline, covering service in the Short Brothers flying boats through to the introduction of the Boeing 707.

This then is that story, produced in the hope that it will have the same reception as its predecessor, *Timber's War*, and will give to those interested, further insight into the thoughts and work of those who 'sit up front'.

CHAPTER 1

IN THE BEGINNING

In anticipation of staying on in the RAF after the war I had applied for, and received, an extended service commission but it soon became evident that the chances of converting this to a permanent commission were extremely remote. For many reasons, other air crew officers had similar aspirations, in spite of the fact that operational flying had prematurely aged those who were fortunate enough to survive the war. Such is the pull of flying which only those involved can really understand.

As a substantive Flight Lieutenant, receiving marriage and other allowances, my salary far exceeded the pittance which the London Office of my pre-war employers were prepared to offer me on my return to civilian life. Quoting the manager of the department in which I had served before the war with the Cunard White Star Shipping Line he said 'We'd be happy to offer you your old job back with the company and allowing for annual increments since you joined the RAF we can now offer you £3 12s 6d per week'.

There is no doubt that these were the words which sent me on my way into a long career in civil aviation.

It was mid-August 1946 and I had just received my demobilisation clothing. Grey chalk-striped suit, herring-bone Raglan style overcoat and a green pork pie hat accompanied by other minor items issued to all servicemen on their return to civilian life, after military service during the 39/45 war.

I counted myself extremely lucky to have survived a tour of operations with Bomber Command in the RAF, followed by a couple of years as an instructor and then an enjoyable and lengthy spell with the long-range VIP flight of Transport Command.

I obviously found myself in a dilemma because the manager of Cunard White Star considered his offer to be more than generous and with a wife and baby to support and no permanent home, since we were living with in-laws, I had to decide whether I should opt for

11

the security of employment with a long-established shipping company and struggle along as best we could or whether I should look elsewhere when, with thousands leaving the services and seeking suitable posts, jobs were very hard to come by.

As so often happened during my career, Providence once again sent an opportunity my way. I had decided to telephone a friend of long standing with whom I had in fact joined the RAF way back in 1939, and during our nostalgic chat I spelled out my problem at length hoping for any suggestion from his end which might take me away from the inevitable miseries and consequences of a lowly paid office life. His response was immediate. 'Aren't you aware that the British Overseas Airways Corporation are crying out for ex-RAF air crew and are interviewing candidates right now.' Having already taken that step himself he gave me a contact telephone number and I broke off the conversation almost immediately in order to telephone British Overseas Airways to see what their Recruitment Department had to say. 'Absolutely no problem,' was the response, when I telephoned with the evidence of the large number of flying hours which I had accumulated with the RAF, the bulk of these being with Transport Command in the later stages of the war. I was immediately asked to report for interview at the London Office of the Airline, close by Green Park Station. I duly presented myself with my flying log books which the interviewing officer scanned briefly. Then having read my service assessments he asked me a few seemingly pertinent questions and stated that if I wished I could be taken on immediately as a second class Navigating Officer. If I accepted, I would join a training course covering the examination subjects which one needed to pass in order to obtain a civil licence and, if successful, I would then be granted a second class civil navigator's licence, that being the minimum qualification required by the Ministry of Aviation in those days, whilst subsequent training and further successful exam results would eventually lead to a first class navigator's licence.

If I remember correctly my initial contract offered £400 a year, or something like that, with annual increments leading up to about £800, with further increases as and when the first class navigator's licence came along.

None of these figures were of immediate interest to me; the most important factor, and my first consideration, being that I now had an opportunity of employment with long-term prospects and could return to an activity which almost anyone who had spent a few thousand hours in the air, and who is really truthful, would admit is beyond comparison.

Many times I had read of people who, elated for one reason or another, walked with a spring in their step, and leaving Stratton House that morning I sensed for the first time the precise nature of that feeling.

My wife was of course delighted at this offer of employment and since it meant a better standard of living than we had at first anticipated she suggested that I accept immediately. Regrettably neither of us was yet aware of the periods of separation which were to follow, when engaged in the long-range flying which was to be a feature of those early pioneering days.

Contracts signed, together with a small group of other 'eager beavers' I was then ordered to report to the headquarters offices at a site on the old Great West Road out of London to be kitted out with company uniforms and from there, a few days later, on to the BOAC training unit at Aldermaston. This being 1946, Aldermaston still functioned as an aerodrome, and the building of the Atomic Research and Development Establishment which now exists there, lay many years ahead. In some ways this move proved to be a form of step back in time for, as we discovered on arrival, the accommodation at Aldermaston fell far short of the standard of service quarters and messes at RAF stations at which many of us had so recently been based. I believe that Aldermaston had been used as a depot or training base for members of the Women's Royal Army Corps, and more than a few of us were shattered at the graffiti left behind by the previous occupants. The very nature of the artwork suggested that it had been placed there by members of the fairer sex, certainly it outdid anything that I had seen before, and I had seen plenty.

On the first day, most of our time was given over to meeting members of the training staff, comprising ground and flying instructors, and in drawing from stores, the personal items of navigation equipment which would be so necessary in the weeks ahead. I was delighted to hear that the flying training would be undertaken in the dear old DC-3 (Douglas Dakota) and would involve a number of European flights.

It was at this stage that I met the indomitable John Sloper, an ex-mariner, who throughout his career with BOAC remained in the training field and was certainly known, and respected, sometimes hated, by almost every incoming trainee for very many years from that time forward.

Lectures took us back over many principles and procedures already known and understood by us veterans, but of course with a bias towards civil requirements which now included astronomical navigation using more advanced sextants than had previously been available to us in the RAF. For reasons, not yet clear, we were required to study the theory of tides and to calculate with great accuracy the high and low tide values for any part of the United Kingdom. I can honestly say that at no time in my career with BOAC, which included over two years operating on the mighty Shorts flying boats, did I ever have cause to use this information. Additionally, we were slowly indoctrinated into the art of spherical trigonometry which would be used in the calculation and application of star observations. Coupled with this, was the use of, and the problems associated with, a marine sextant. Why this, we wondered, and needless to say, I never had occasion to use a marine sextant nor, to the best of my knowledge, did the airline possess one. Many years later I realised that this requirement stemmed solely from the fact that early Ministry of Aviation examiners were ex-mariners and this explained the reason.

Of course astronomical navigation is now a thing of the past, as far as aviation is concerned, and even when used by mariners today the information is processed through pre-programmed portable computers to provide rapid results. When I consider the cumbersome systems which we were required to use and look at the massive volumes of tabulations, which incidentally I still have in my bookcase, I can see why, until we became familiar with the procedures, we wondered how on earth we should ever be able to cope in the air.

As an example of what we saw as useless knowledge, one examination question suggested that a marine sextant had been used to measure the angle between two stars. The examinee was asked to calculate the true angle between the stars, using spherical trigonometry, and then the true and theoretical angles were compared in order to establish the sextant error. All of this for an airborne navigator, I ask you! Incidentally this was only a small part of the theoretical knowledge required in one of about eight examination subjects. I might add, in conclusion, that the dreaded marine sextant required a visible horizon, which rarely existed in true form in the air. Thank goodness great progress had been made by then in the development of bubble sextants which required no visible horizon and relied on a form of spirit level to produce vertical and horizontal references, at the same time giving greater accuracy, since they were capable of producing a reliable mean value for a series of observations.

Unlike our early training days in the RAF, we now had quite a few flying hours under our belts, which led to a great deal of questioning of the Company's procedures and practices. However, maturity overcame cockiness, and we began to see the wisdom of the advice being meted out, particularly since a fair measure of it came from older hands, some more operationally qualified than ourselves.

The challenge of once again taking and passing examinations was soon upon us and I must add, that the rigid control and high standards applied by the Ministry of Aviation examiners was frightening to say the least. However, success was essential and so we were obliged to go along with the system and its somewhat over-bureaucratic requirements. In the period, whilst awaiting results, we were prepared for our training flights in Dakotas, the general idea being that on each overseas flight the outbound sector would be a familiarisation flight, thereby enabling the trainee to operate the homebound flight as part of the overall testing procedure.

I note with interest, that of the four sectors which I operated whilst training, three resulted in diversions from the destination, due to poor weather.

On 10 December 1946, resplendent in navy-blue uniform with sleeves heavily braided to signify my new found rank of Navigating Officer Second Class, I joined a small group of students and tutors, covering each of the normal flight crew categories, in order to position our Dakota aircraft at London (Heathrow) Airport, known simply then as London Airport. This was essential since all overseas departures had to be cleared through a Customs controlled airport.

Although I had received a brief rundown on the navigation equipment in the Dakota, I was pleasantly surprised to find that, unlike the RAF versions which had been stripped of most of the interior trim for obvious reasons, I now sat in a comfortably cushioned seat, with soundproof padding covering the airframe interior and instruments which had all the hallmarks of thoughtful design and presentation, far removed from our recently experienced, very basic, British versions.

London Airport in those days was in the early stages of development with a single runway and a collection of portable buildings clustered on the north side and sited round one of the old RAF brick-built control towers, which housed most of the operational briefing departments.

Trooping into the meteorological section, we were informed that it was already snowing at our planned destination in Stockholm, with little chance of any clearance for some while. Our skipper, one of the many veterans on the BOAC payroll, simply shrugged his shoulders and said 'We'll have a shot at it anyway'.

A description of in-flight procedures doesn't really matter at this stage, suffice it to say that half an hour out of Stockholm we had a message to say that the aerodrome was closed due to heavy snowfalls and a build-up of snow on the runway. What to do now? Our skipper, a man of decision, not to be denied a night away from home, elected to head for Gothenberg and there we spent the night. I remember little of where we stayed or what we did, apart from the fact that we drank some form of local brew to excess and paid for it with king-sized hangovers the next day. However, it was a short run home and we had only ourselves to care for on the aircraft.

Christmas intervened before my next flight and we were granted leave, to return to duty in the New Year of 1947. On 7 January, oddly enough in the same aircraft which I am sure was 'jinxed', I set off on my second indoctrination flight. This time to Gibraltar with the prospect of returning home laden with duty free goods. A popular flight to say the least, but on which all went haywire once again. We had departed from London Airport around midday following, oddly enough, the same coast-crawling route which I had been used to in my last months in the RAF. This amounted to crossing the Bay of Biscay to Cape Finisterre and thence due south with the Spanish and Portuguese coasts in sight, most of the way, when cloud permitted.

Turning south-east from Cape St Vincent, and with light beginning to fade, I noted frantic handwritten messages passing between the radio officer and the captain, concluding with the words which, politely translated, amounted to 'Oh goodness me, why should it happen to us', from the latter. Apparently the dear old Rock was covered by low cloud, with drizzle and a crosswind on the runway.

All thoughts of cheap booze and a night out on the town were forgotten in the haste to find an alternative aerodrome, but with a flash of brilliance, the skipper said, 'Why not Lisbon?' Why not indeed, it probably had more to offer than Gibraltar, as far as our uncultured tastes were concerned.

It was by now getting dark and as we turned tail in a north-westerly direction, the instructor insisted that I set up the sextant and take a few star observations in order to check our position. I could have slaughtered the man, for as we moved westwards, coastal lights and towns gave a clear indication of where we were and indeed, for some considerable distance out from Lisbon, the sky was well lit by the great city lights.

No problems with landing at a strange aerodrome since it was a major airport, and local staff having already received word of our diversion from Gibraltar, had sorted out reasonable hotel accommodation.

We were able to make most of the purchases which we had planned for in Gibraltar, coupled with one or two unexpected ones and at the crack of dawn we were off back to London.

An hour out from our destination the jinx struck again and we had a radio message to say that the weather at London Airport had fallen below our permitted landing limits and we were to divert to Croydon, of all places, the reason being that it was the nearest available Customs airport to London. So my short spell of training ended and we now returned to further practical studies and to await our examination results.

They came through soon enough and thanks to a combination of past experience, determination and first-class instruction we all made the grade and after the paperwork had been completed, held that treasured document the flight navigator's licence in our hands. I suppose I should have added the words 'second-class', as there was more to follow. Just as in the RAF, everyone was on edge, wondering where the next stage of our careers would take us, with most hopes set on the prestigious North Atlantic run. In due course, our marching orders arrived, and I was called in to the chief instructor's office, full of apprehension, further aggravated by the glum expression on his face as I entered.

'Sorry "Timber" you've lost out on the Atlantic posting but you're going to Hythe, to Number Four Line.' Each unit in those days, had a 'Line' number.

Hythe, the penny dropped and my spirits rose. This was the flying boat base on Southampton Water, a posting I hardly dreamed would come my way one day.

Many were the films, photographs and books that I had studied in the past, telling of the routes flown by these giants and of the exotic places which they visited and now quite unexpectedly it was all coming my way. In fact, four of us had been selected for this posting and in each case the North Atlantic route was immediately forgotten.

Details followed quickly and with a short break of a few days, we were briefed to report to the 'Line' headquarters at the main base at Hythe on the west side of Southampton Water, where another course of training had been laid on for us, this time to familiarise us with the route and aircraft but more importantly to study the examination subjects which were required for a first-class navigators licence, that being a prerequisite before commencing 'Line' operations.

CHAPTER 2

JOINING THE WEB-FOOTED

This posting meant, of course, that I should have to uproot myself from the home which my wife and I had established with our first child in my wife's parents' home, and find accommodation in the vicinity of Hythe, certainly for the period of concentrated study which was to follow. I did not realise it at that time, but ahead of me lay long periods of absence from home, for in those days it was not uncommon to spend a month away whilst 'pounding' the Far Eastern routes.

Fortunately, for both of us, my wife had spent most of the war years in the WAAF and this grounding made her more than able to cope with running a home whilst the boss was away. Or was the boss really at home?

Arriving at Southampton, I boarded the ageing Hythe ferry for the trip across the Solent and shortly after leaving the town pier, I had my first sight of the giant flying boats ahead. Some were beached awaiting servicing at the base whilst others swayed gently in the swell, downcurrent from their mooring buoys. I don't have the descriptive ability to convey the effect of this first sighting, but anyone who recalls these gentle giants will know the visual impact. Flying boats had been linked with this part of the world for many years. Further down the Solent the RAF had used the marine base at Calshot, where coupled with the Supermarine (Vickers) Limited Company, record-breaking seaplanes had been flown to capture the Schneider Trophy time and time again.

I think it was in 1937 that regular flying boat services were first operated by Imperial Airways out of Southampton, using the famous 'C' Class Empire flying boats built by Shorts of Rochester. They flew the East and Central African routes terminating at Durban but additionally, proving flights were undertaken to Botwood in Newfoundland, via Foynes, the marine base near Limerick in Western Ireland.

The Eastern routes were slowly extended and pushed farther and farther east to Karachi, Singapore, and eventually right through to Sydney. When Italy entered the war the European sectors were killed off but this led to the opening up of the famous horseshoe route, when flying boats were operated through from Durban via East Africa to India and then on down through Malaya to Australia. Of course the Far Eastern war finally put paid to that route also, although attempts were made to bypass war zones both in Europe and the East.

In 1940, Imperial Airways was absorbed by the British Overseas Airways Corporation (BOAC), who promptly set up the marine base at Poole Harbour.

A few flying boats were loaned to the RAF and some were lost, but in 1943, a number of ex-RAF Sunderlands were converted for civilian use by Shorts of Rochester and rechristened as 'Hythes'. These aircraft enabled BOAC to re-open the service from Poole to Karachi and later, when more converted boats arrived in 1944, this route was extended to Calcutta. Slowly but surely the route was extended further east until finally in 1946, it reached Sydney and BOAC had by then taken over and re-opened the original Empire routes. Shorts did eventually produce a full civilian version of the Sunderland which became known as the Sandringham. Other versions of the Sunderland were also produced by Shorts, to be known as Solents and Plymouths and finally with this mix of all classes, BOAC was able in 1948 to extend its routes right up into Japan.

Disembarking from the ferry, I made my way to the base headquarters to join other new arrivals. We were first advised to obtain accommodation in Southampton, as it was at a premium in Hythe, but we were helped with a list of suitable landladies. For convenience I paired off with Tony 'C' another navigator, and we contacted and settled for a Mrs 'B' who resided in the suburb of Shirley.

Known as 'Ma' to all her residents she provided a home from home with the finest cooking it has ever been my good fortune to enjoy. Her husband, the 'Boss', was in fact the captain of, if that is the right word, the giant floating crane which operated along the South Coast and was known as the 'London Mammoth'. What an odd character he was. A very light sleeper, who when we crept out at night in response to nature's call, insisted on coughing loudly, either to remind us that he was awake too, or that we had awoken him. It was all very disturbing and in the end led to enforced bladder control. Tony and I added pounds to our weight as a consequence of Ma's cooking but it made life pleasant whilst away from home.

We worked very hard at the base and in due course sat and passed the necessary examinations thereby making us immediately available for route operations. In those days, there were no flights to be made under supervision. Once rostered for flying you were on your own, although of course this did not apply to pilots.

What a fine body of men those early captains were, almost every one a character in his own right, with more eccentrics than I had ever met before. As this tale progresses I will highlight more of their eccentricities, characteristics, and whims or whatever else it was that separated one from another.

To my delight I was advised that on 23 March 1947 I was to join Captain Brand and crew to operate out to Singapore, Bangkok and Hong Kong, over a period of the next three weeks. I hastened home to make suitable arrangements covering my absence and on the night before departure made my way to the Harbour Heights Hotel in Poole (Dorset). This hotel provided accommodation for passengers and crew overnight and had them ready and on the spot for an early departure the following morning. I say on the spot, because although the aircraft were based and serviced at Hythe, they operated out of Poole Harbour with the Yacht Club as a base for crews and staff. It was at least a year or more before cost cutting forced BOAC to concentrate all activities from Southampton Water alone.

With an early call, followed by a cup of tea, I hastened to don my brand-new, almost navy style uniform, with its broad gold braid rank markings and made my way somewhat self-consciously to join the rest of the crew for breakfast and then the transport to the Yacht Club.

The crew immediately recognised me as a new boy, and they were extremely friendly and helpful and why not, since we had three weeks of close contact ahead of us. The skipper, Ted Brand, was the first of the many characters I was to meet in the months ahead, and at first glance he appeared quite elderly after the young men I had so recently flown with in the RAF. This was not surprising since many of the captains had been flying these mighty monsters from the early Empire flying boat days or were veterans of the Coastal Command of the Royal Air Force.

Discipline was very strong and there was never any suggestion of undue familiarity with the skipper as he was truly the Boss. The crew transport dropped us at the Yacht Club where a civilian weather forecaster gave us a run down on what we were to expect between Poole and the destination for that day which was the Bay of Augusta, south of Catania in Sicily, with a refuelling stop on the way at the huge Lake Marignane, adjacent to Marseille.

No computers in those days. The navigator was handed a weather forecast and then sat down and methodically calculated the compass headings required and the estimated time, for each of the sectors which made up the full route to Marseille.

Ted was no respecter of pedantic or nitpicking perfectionists and I was told to hurry it up. 'We don't really need all this,' he said, 'I can get there alone without a bloody navigator.' I confess to being very downhearted at this stage, as I was doing my best to impress, but the smile on his face and the quick wink, put me immediately at ease. Then into the crew launch for the quick trip out to the aircraft.

As I have already explained, the types of flying boats operated by BOAC varied, although they were all variants of the Short Sunderland. On this occasion we were operating a Hythe III variant, powered by Bristol Pegasus 48 engines, and with the given name of *Hotspur*. All Hythes carried a name commencing with the letter H.

As we ran alongside, prior to boarding, I realised for the first time just how immense these aircraft were, and as one stepped on board, it was like stepping into a different world. The lower deck was divided into a number of different compartments, each containing six or eight lounge style chairs with an adjacent table and, of course, a window alongside. Depending on the type of aircraft one might find an observation lounge, a bar, and on later types an upper deck with sleeping accommodation. Moving forward, out of the passenger accommodation one came to a section which, in the military version would have housed a gun turret, but in civilian versions provided a removable mooring hatch and bollard, used by the radio officer whose duty it was to handle the slipping and mooring procedures. The crew had to climb a step ladder up into the top level, where, after crossing the main wingspar, they arrived on the flight deck. From the navigator's point of view it was heaven. On the port (left) side and behind the captain's seat he was provided with a huge oblong chart table, the like of which I had never seen before.

Preparing a flying boat for take-off is in many ways similar to the procedure needed for handling a large boat, certainly in the initial stages. For my part, my duty was to withdraw the Perspex upper hatch and take in the various flags and pennants. Two small removable stub masts were fitted either side of the aircraft and we were required to fly the BOAC house flag, the airmail pennant and the national flag of the country, wherever we might be. National flags were stowed in pockets on the flight deck, but one had to be very careful in selecting and hoisting them after landing. This was because some of the wags in our midst had a habit of changing them around, and you may rest assured that it is no fun to have a police launch come alongside to complain that you were flying the flag of Pakistan, when you had just landed on the Nile in Egypt. I then had to help keep a watchful eye from the astro (Perspex) dome in case there was any conflicting traffic around. During preparations, the passenger launch or launches would come alongside and the catering staff would greet passengers and assist them to their seats.

Once the radio officer had positioned himself in the open forward hatch, armed with a boat-hook, the captain would commence the starting procedure.

I should mention that the minimum crew consisted of the captain, a co-pilot or first officer, occasionally a third pilot or second officer, a navigator, radio officer and engineer. Catering staff varied in number and appointment over the years. Pursers controlled passenger care in the early days, but later on, the title of steward was fully adopted by all catering staff with the very junior newcomers being appointed as catering apprentices. It was quite some time before we welcomed ladies to our catering section on the aircraft but it was a great day indeed when they did arrive.

Usually, the flying boat would be floating downstream linked to a buoy by a mooring rope, so that once the engines had been started the aircraft could be eased gently forward, thus enabling the radio officer to slip and drop the mooring rope from the aircraft bollard and then we were away. In slipping, or mooring, it often became necessary to use the familiar canvas 'wind sock' type of drogue or sea anchor. This could be used to produce a turn against the tide or the wind and whatever control was demanded of these drogues was achieved by the use of commands from the captain using a metal whistle. I hasten to add that many were the times when failure of the radio officer to respond to these whistled commands led to an outburst of strong language from the skipper which more than compensated and certainly produced the desired results.

The stories of mishaps to radio officers, whilst assisting with the mooring, are legion, and most conclude with those fine chaps disappearing over the side with boat-hook in hand. Occasionally approaching a mooring, and failing to take note of a command from the captain to ignore a particular buoy when he wished to move ahead to another, the mooring line was duly attached by the radio officer, whilst the boat under the captain's control moved ahead only to be brought to a violent stop as the 'unwanted' mooring rope, now looped from the wrong buoy, took up the strain. It certainly caused the nose to dip and the tail to rise in a frightening manner and frequently provided an outburst of expletives from the flight deck. It was all quite entertaining and led to some wonderful verbal exchanges, always with superior rank in mind of course. Amazing what a radio officer could say to a captain, without insolence or disrespect, but still with maximum effect, 'Sorry sir, I didn't realise that you couldn't cope with that buoy'!

Starting procedure usually began with the starboard (right) outer engine and moved right to left across the wing until all four Pegasus engines were rumbling away. On more than one occasion a starter motor failed to work and then one of the great assets of this mighty machine came to the fore. Armed with a suitable tool or maybe only using his boot, the flight engineer would open the roof hatch and cautiously walk along the wing, to give the faulty starter motor a resounding whack through the engine casing. In most cases this freed the tardy starter and away went the engine.

All engines now running with a reassuring purr and with a signal from the launch, and over the radio, that the take-off area was free of vessels, the radio officer was given the order, or whistle, to slip the mooring rope, and having done so and closed the mooring hatch the gentle giant moved slowly forward through the water towards the start of take-off point. Whilst approaching this point full engine checks were carried out and the radio officer opened up on the appropriate radio frequency, using morse code procedures, since this was the main means of long-range communication in those days.

All checks proving satisfactory and all hatches closed, a gentle turn into the take-off direction and then on with the power for take-off.

To the uninitiated this could be a frightening experience at the best of times, because not only was the first need to overcome inertia since the hull was firmly settled into the water, but there was also a need to gain sufficient speed to get the boat up on to the 'step' and then to unstick the hull from the water, when by virtue of a vacuum effect it was disinclined to do so. Study of a flying boat hull when it is out of the water reveals the construction of the 'step', but until this stage is reached at take-off the step is far from apparent.

In the first stages of take-off, a tremendous amount of water is displaced and the passengers' view is blotted out by masses of water and spray thundering by. Once on the 'step', the boat takes on the feel of a fast-moving high-powered racing boat and the main disturbance of water is then concentrated in the massive wake. As the speed builds up, there is a wonderful feeling of elation, that such a giant should suddenly become so sleek as it tops the water, before with a final easing back on the control column, she moves slowly but gracefully into the air.

I won't pretend that the Hythe was a quiet aircraft, far from it, because we had none of the refinements of modern-day aircraft to minimise the noise and a large area of the flight deck was simply metal frame supporting large areas of Perspex window.

On the morning of this my first flight a region of high pressure had settled over Western Europe and calm conditions prevailed, leading inevitably to fog as we climbed slowly out, heading in a southerly direction. I passed the required compass headings to Ted Brand, noting as I did so, the 'Old Harry' headland near Swanage passing slowly by on the starboard side.

My next duty was to prepare an information card for circulation to the passengers, showing the route we were to follow, and places of interest with approximate times of passing. At this point I met up with the first idiosyncrasy of one of these boat characters. Easing himself out of his seat and reaching down into a small box, the skipper produced a portable typewriter, and without apology or explanation slapped it down on the centre of my carefully prepared chart.

'Right, let's have the information and I'll do the job properly,' said he. Somewhat hurt that I should not be trusted with such an easy task so early in the flight, I made my feelings known in a polite way. With a wry smile, Ted said 'Don't upset yourself, I always do it this way.'

Perhaps I should have done what many navigators are alleged to have done, in the past, when thoughtless crew members placed anything from coffee cups to larger items on the chart table without any thought of the disturbance which it could cause to a conscientious navigator. The answer to this problem was to hand the captain a request for an unrealistic and massive change in compass heading and when this was queried, to say that you were merely navigating around the coffee cup or whatever.

The Channel and French Coast were shrouded in mist but I caught a quick glimpse of the Seine which confirmed that we were pretty well on the required track.

Of course, in 1947, there was no vast network of airways or an air traffic control system to monitor progress and one simply flew as close as possible to the sectors or legs as they were known. Flight planned data had previously been calculated and filed at the departure point.

Our cruising height was around 9,000 feet, and since the Hythe was really not up to safely crossing the Alps or even the high ground to the east of the Rhône Valley our route was planned just east of south, the highest ground en route then being the Cévennes.

Settling down at cruising height I was able to make use of a few of the radio beacons which had been established across France and thereby obtain a reasonable position check. The mist still lay well below and in some places was obviously down to ground level since trees and buildings could occasionally be seen jutting up through.

About an hour and a half out, things brightened up a little as the early morning fog was obviously being slowly burned off by the sun and there ahead lay the broad sweep of the River Loire. No problem with map reading here, with easily recognisable stretches of the river and the large cities of Tours and Blois either side of our track. Crossing our track at right angles the river provided an excellent check on our groundspeed, that is our speed over the ground as distinct from through the air, the difference being governed by the windspeed and direction at our altitude. Being an anticyclonic situation there was in fact little wind effect and both of these speeds were, as near as makes no difference, the same.

Looking ahead I was disturbed to see a sheet of cloud, presumably lifted fog, as far as the eye could see. However, the radio officer who had been hammering away at his morse key without a break had received coded weather information from Marseille indicating clear conditions, but with a strong northerly wind for landing at Marignane. The northerly wind known as the Mistral was produced by the funnel effect of the Rhône Valley which simply channelled the air flow down the Valley and out into the Mediterranean.

At this stage of the flight, I learned of one of the very useful landmarks known to veteran captains, who from sitting up front had grown to recognise these from vast distances. On seeing my consternation, when I came forward between the pilots' seats to look ahead for a visual check only to be greeted by solid cloud below, Ted said 'Don't worry we're bang on track'. Far too polite to question his statement, I looked ahead for evidence, and there it was. Jutting out from cloud and sitting on top of a hill some 4,000 feet in height, was the Monastery of Le Puy, which a quick check from the map revealed should be just to the right of our track, as indeed it obviously was. Passing it on our beam, I had the track check I needed, and with the time and distance since crossing the Loire I now had a fresh check on the groundspeed.

Very many times in the future, weather conditions permitting, I found that I could relax a little, if and when I had the monastery in sight, however far off.

The weather did indeed clear progessively and apart from a measure of turbulence as we crossed the high ground of the Cévennes we broke into clear Mediterranean sunshine in the region of Nîmes, whence with a slight change in heading we closed in on Marseille. Descending rapidly we obtained clearance to land, but were warned that the wind was very strong and gusting over the lake. As we made a circuit, the white caps on Lake Marignane confirmed that the surface was very choppy, always a danger because with chop or swell, it was possible to misjudge the landing and a dipped wing could cost you a float, but more of that later. With an experienced captain and a wind which was certainly steady in direction, if not in speed, we touched down safely on to a very choppy surface. At this stage it was necessary to disembark passengers as quickly as possible, lest they and their expensive airborne meals should part company, but we immediately hit a problem.

With the very strong wind, we could not turn to head back across the Lake to our mooring point. The massive rudder surface acted almost like a sail and any attempt to turn across wind simply shifted the tail back again coupled with which there was a danger that such a wind, if it caught us in the middle of a turn, could cause a wing to dip with the possibility of losing or maybe holing, a wing float.

So on the first leg of my first trip, I had to assist in sailing this great flying boat backwards. Standing with my head through the open roof hatch, I had to report on backward progress to the captain, as the rudder was virtually used as a sail to take us back. It was a fine piece of manouvring on the captain's part as he used the engines to correct any tendency to swing one way or another, until we moved into calmer waters, whereupon the various launches did their bit to turn us and head us towards our mooring buoy.

Speaking to the passengers that night, I found that most of them saw this as a unique event, great fun – as one old lady put it, little understanding what had really happened or rather what had nearly happened. Once 'on the buoy', passengers were disembarked and we followed shortly after, having left instructions for refuelling and departure requirements for the next sector.

After a brief snack in the adjacent restaurant we were informed that all was ready and so we, together with our passengers, were transported rapidly to the lakeside. It was a choppy ride in the launch out to our aircraft and just a trifle difficult to board as the giant was wallowing badly in the roughish water, although we could see that it was much worse farther out in the lake.

However, with the strong northerly wind we were able to start up, slip the mooring and start the take-off run almost from the buoy. It was a comparatively short take-off run but rather uncomfortable and with the choppy water the early stages suggested we were running over an unending stretch of cobblestones. Once airborne we turned off towards the south-east, with a forecast, as best we could understand from the Frenchman at Marseille, of part cloud conditions with a possible build up into showers or thunderstorms over Corsica and Sardinia. Most people associate fine weather with the Mediterranean but I can assure them that in spring and autumn, at about the change of season, the weather can be as bad as that suffered in the United Kingdom – indeed the thunderstorms can often be worse.

We made a long slow climb up to around 10,000 feet, for although our route was planned to take us through the Straits of Bonifacio, between Corsica and Sardinia, we had to bear in mind that should we find ourselves in cloud and possibly without an accurate check on position there was a danger of drifting towards Monte Cinto, the highest point in Corsica which was some 9,000 feet in height.

Fortunately we found well-broken cloud with a somewhat murky sea somewhere below and not long after leaving the Riviera behind we could see the mass of cumulus cloud ahead which was obviously sitting on the high ground over both islands. A break between the masses suggested that the Strait was below and sure enough there it was. With sunshine above a break in the cumulus cloud I was able to obtain an accurate position check, after which we again passed out over the Mediterranean for the sea crossing to Sicily.

Fortunately, being so soon after the war, some of the high powered radio beacons were still operating in that part of the world and it was not unduly difficult to fix our position by a series of accurate radio position lines.

Once firmly established on the correct track, I was allowed to go below for a short spell to observe, and chat to, the passengers. Comfortably settled in cosy seats and compartments and with a good lunch and wine inside them, they were all most amenable and fired off many questions about the aircraft, the route and the night stop station ahead. I confess, this being my first trip, that I was more than cautious with my responses whilst still trying to convey the impression of being a veteran flying boat navigator, hopefully without revealing the true situation. I then returned to the flight deck as soon as possible.

Our approach to Sicily was via Palermo on the north-western tip of the island, and as the weather became progressively clearer, the rocky coastline and adjacent headlands could be seen. Far ahead, was the impressive sight of Mount Etna and, with its height and adjacent turbulence in mind, we tracked along the north coast, to pass Etna on our right and once well clear, turned south towards our destination.

The bay at Augusta was ideal as an alighting area with adequate take-off and landing runs in all directions and complete shelter from any outside disturbances. It so happened that on that particular day a unit of the American Fleet was in the port and included the giant aircraft carrier USS *Forrestal.* We were delighted to receive an invitation to visit them that evening since they were as impressed with our flying boat as we were with their naval vessels. It was an interesting visit, but I seem to recall that it was a 'dry' one too.

The landing at Augusta gave no problems and as a new flying boat dock had just been installed we disembarked comfortably and in a straightforward manner. Several of these docks had been set up along the route wherever possible and proved to be of great benefit. The flying boat had to be moored in the usual way, normally on to a buoy adjacent to the dock, and then by the use of a tail line the flying boat was towed gently backwards between two pontoon-style platforms, thus enabling all and sundry to walk off.

Accommodation at Augusta consisted of pretty substantial rooms in a large house, converted almost hotel style, and the whole unit was run by the ebullient 'Bunny' Austin, another character, if ever I met one. Over the years, I heard endless stories of Bunny's activities, adventures and financial deals but whatever may have been said, nothing besmirched his fair name and although he often disappeared from one station or another it was only a question of time before he popped up again. I recall bumping into him in places as far apart as the Victoria Falls Hotel and then shortly after at the Beach Club at Accra. Forever in charge and seemingly always doing a great job, he certainly had something to offer to BOAC, for how else could he have existed and survived as long as he did, up and down the many airways routes?

CHAPTER 3

ONWARD AND EASTWARD

A ugusta was just a very comfortable and quiet spot at which to rest overnight, although occasional visits to Taormina, a pleasant little resort to the north, returning with sore heads attributable to too much Marsala, did sometimes liven things up a little. Doubtless some airborne mariners will still remember the train rides back from Taormina with frantic attempts on the part of the driver to prevent us from taking over his job on the return journey.

An early call, a substantial breakfast and then we were off on our way to the next night stop at Cairo. This sector was pretty boring as the whole flight was over the sea and the navigation consisted in the main of using radio beacons.

This was a fairly new facility in the Eastern Mediterranean since a number of the higher powered radio transmitters had only recently come back on the air again after the war. Fortunately the flying boats still retained an old fashioned drift recorder and by studying the wind direction, visible as 'wind lanes' across the surface of the sea and combining this with the angle at which the aircraft was drifting, it was possible to determine the windspeed and direction at the lower levels. Armed with this information a reasonably accurate compass heading could be calculated and used thereafter.

Inevitably, and to keep one's hand in, some use was made of the sextant and certainly the position lines obtained from the sun and occasionally the moon in daylight, gave good navigational support. So for some six hours, and without too many weather problems, the flight progressed routinely until the Egyptian coastline east of Mersa Matruh hove into sight.

Not too difficult to obtain a visual fix but in any event, with the radio compass tuned into the very powerful directional beacon sited by the Americans at an airfield in the Suez Canal zone, the run into Cairo presented no problems. The alighting area on the Nile was to the north of the city of Cairo at Rod El Farag and had to be very carefully monitored by our own marine staff.

Launches were sent out shortly before landing to warn the river traffic to hold off and of course they were well aware of our needs, but no sooner had the area been cleared than the odd felucca or two would attempt to sneak across. The felucca incidentally, was a medium sized, almost barge style vessel, with a large lateen sail, to be found in large numbers transporting their goods and wares up and down the Nile.

As a problem, it could be handled in daylight but occasionally we were faced with a night landing at Cairo. The flare path would be set out using a line of small dinghies, originally fitted with flares, but subsequently with battery powered lights and feluccas duly warned off ahead of our approach. If a 'landing' had to be made to the north, the final approach was over a large girdered railway bridge, then almost swooping down on to the water after we had crossed it. As a result on more than one occasion a felucca attempted to sneak across the alighting area and lost part of its main mast, fortunately without damage to the aircraft which had struck it. One certainly had to be vigilant on the approach, particularly since the 'locals' did not have the same regard for safety as we professional airmen.

At Rod El Farag, mooring was to a buoy with disembarkation by launch, which then took us to the jetty, where moored nearby, was a river houseboat which provided crew and passengers with their night-stop accommodation. I cannot recall the name of this particular boat but understand that many years earlier it had been operated by Thomas Cook, the travel agent, in the far off days when Nile travel was an expensive but satisfactory way of holiday-making.

Unfortunately, this houseboat had seen better days although most of the cabins were reasonably comfortable. I have reason to remember one mark of this vessel's age when I had decided to take a bath that evening. The bath was an ancient free-standing Victorian style vessel with huge brass taps looking as though they required a spanner to operate them. In the twilight, I looked for the light control and there on the cabin wall alongside the bath was a huge brass switch, with a loose screw-on cap, hanging down from the small switch arm. Why it hadn't fallen off I simply do not know. Stupidly I reached up to screw on the cap before operating the switch and then it happened. What precisely I can only assume, but all I remember is coming to, in the bath, with a dreadful pain in my right arm. The truth dawned immediately and although further details do not matter I would not be telling this story had the supply been more than 110 volts.

Badly shaken, I joined the crew for our evening meal and dropped the subject of the light switch when to a man they denied me all sympathy and simply condemned my stupidity, which I guess was fair comment. There was no form of entertainment on the houseboat and insufficient time to visit the city of Cairo since another early start lay ahead of us on the morrow, so we sat on the afterdeck supping the local brew whilst bargaining with the on-board shopkeeper whose main wares seemed to consist of a wide variety of dirty postcards.

I guess due to a combination of relief and fatigue, I slept right through my first night on the houseboat until the room boy came along with the mandatory morning cup of tea.

Once more an early start as we had two sectors to complete on this day, a six-and-a-half hour flight across the desert to Basra on the Shatt al Arab pretty well at the confluence of the Rivers Tigris and Euphrates, followed by a bumpy ride down the Persian Gulf for a night stop at Bahrain.

After departing from Cairo we followed a northerly track before turning east across the desert. In later days, with more powerful high flying aircraft the initial route then took us south across 'Aqaba, since the aeroplanes could then cope with crossing the mountainous terrain which bordered the eastern side of the Gulf of 'Aqaba.

In the late forties, it was usual to obtain as high a cruising altitude as possible to avoid the dreadful turbulence which boiled up, once the sun got to work on the desert sand. However, since luxuries such as pressurisation, and unlimited oxygen if and when required, lay many years ahead, there was a limit to our cruising height, and many an expensive passenger lunch went down and then returned again, on this sector.

Taken overall, it is true to say that it was usually a rather unpleasant few hours, with little to help with navigation, once the Jordan Valley and surrounding hills had been left behind. Long before oil exploration got underway on a grand scale, the original pipeline joining the Mediterranean outlet to the oil fields at Mosul and Kirkūk provided a very useful line to follow, always provided the aircraft was flying along the northern edge of the desert. This pipeline and the adjoining road or track running alongside it was well marked and if no sandstorms were blowing, was usually clearly visible. Added to this a few very primitive landing strips, with the landing area marked out in oil, provided a very useful aid to mark progress along the track. Oil was used since once sprayed on to the surface, the sun very quickly baked it into an almost tar-like surface.

Unfortunately, as our track on this occasion was to Basra, and not further north to Baghdad, we were left with a crossing of the bleak almost featureless Arabian Desert.

I have always found it difficult to describe these vast desert regions as seen from the air, because, cloud conditions permitting, as far as the eye can see there is nothing but sheer wasteland. Far from being a mass of one colour, there are many colours all stemming from the sand dunes, rock outcrops and dried up wadis or one-time river beds. Having said that, it still remains featureless from the navigator's point of view. Maps were pretty useless as the areas had yet to be fully surveyed from the air and the only sign of life, which was visible if one really concentrated, would be the occasional cluster of black Bedouin tents. What these Nomads did and where they were going was anybody's guess.

There was however one useful checkpoint on the direct track to Basra, and that was somewhere near the desert centre. This was the oasis of Al Jawf. I never had the good fortune to see this spot at close range, but it stood out from afar as a darkish patch, presumably date palms, in the otherwise brown and yellow landscape. A comforting sight, a useful check on progress eastwards, and invaluable as an aid to revising the arrival time if necessary.

In previous years, I had become accustomed to the difficulties of map-reading when approaching the marsh area north of Basra, since in RAF days we had landed at Shaibah, an RAF staging post airfield just to the north. There were so many small loops and whorls in the Euphrates that it took some time to sort one out from another, but now we had the luxury of a radio beacon at Basra and the fact that whatever happened there was a lot of water upon which we could alight. In later years I shared many hairy flights into this area, when visibility went down almost to zero in sandstorms, or rising dust as they were called. On this occasion, all was well and after the usual approach formalities, Ted Brand settled the giant bird down on to the river and we were all offloaded whilst the refuelling barge came alongside to top up our tanks.

A refreshing drink and back to the launch again to embark ready for the next short sector to Bahrain.

In those days the ground crews, headed by efficient station

managers, were very proud of the speed with which they were able to receive and despatch aircraft and remember this included launch trips to and from the flying boat into the bargain. The station manager, resplendent in tropical uniform, was inevitably there with a smart salute to greet the captain and woe betide him if he were not. However that was in the happy days of super efficiency and pride in work. The support officers were there too, and for my part, it was nice to be greeted by an operations officer with a fully prepared flight plan for the next sector, which merely required a quick check, before confirming the fuel uplift required. Quite often the engineering officer would remain on board to see that all ran smoothly although on most occasions it did anyway.

The flight down the Gulf in what was now late afternoon, was turbulent, to say the least, in spite of the fact that it was conducted mainly over the sea. We tended to fly just offshore so that navigation was no great problem as the irregular shape of the coastline in places made map-reading very easy.

Kuwait lay well off to the right, but of course in those days it was no more than a large fishing port. Certainly no high rise buildings and the only evidence of events to come was a single, very long, jetty running out to supply the tankers offshore. Further down the coast towards Bahrain the Americans had been working hard on oil extraction at Dhahran on the Arabian mainland and a large storage centre was also being developed at the prominent headland of Ras Tanura.

Bahrain airfield is sited on the island of Muharraq which is joined to the main island of Manamah by a causeway and our alighting area was in effect between the two. I had stayed at Bahrain on numerous occasions whilst flying with the RAF, although in those days our accommodation was undoubtedly as primitive as any I had ever seen. Things were to be different now, although one thing had not changed nor ever will. As we descended on our approach, the side windows were opened and the hot air blasted in as if from a furnace.

Touch down on the clear almost blue water was smooth, but pretty well forgotten as the hot sticky humid air engulfed everything. Perspiration poured off everyone and there was nothing to be done except to suffer until relief was obtained when we finally arrived at our night stop centre.

BOAC had acquired a so called rest house, later to be developed into a hotel, which really was the Hilton of its day, so much so that, partly because Arabia was dry, and partly because of its reasonable comfort, the American 'oily boys' from Dhahran, frequently came across for a break. The rest house was run by a certain station manager named Parker, who became a legend in those parts for reasons which do not matter, and he certainly made a good job of it.

The rest house was on a par with some of the smaller Indian hotels and over the years the room equipment developed from the old-fashioned ceiling fans through portable air conditioners finally to full air conditioning, hence real comfort was provided by BOAC on this small oven-like island.

The bar was the focal point for evening socialising, and from amongst the many American visitors, all oil men, I met some of strangest, brashest, 'odd balls' it has ever been my good fortune to run into. I never did find out how one of these chaps managed to acquire a live green parrot which accompanied him wherever he went and was perched on the top of his ten gallon hat. He conversed regularly with the bird, but since he was rarely sober and the bird couldn't understand a word he was saying, it simply screeched back at him. I don't really know what level of understanding existed between them but there must have been some because they seemed to dwell quite happily together. On one occasion I met him at the bar on what must have been an off day for the parrot. The 'cowboy' was grumbling away in his beer and when I asked him what was wrong he replied 'I'm, going to ring that goddam parrot's neck, the bastard hasn't said a word to me all day'.

I have no idea who this character was or where he laboured, if he laboured at all, but invariably when we passed through Bahrain he'd be present at the bar. There was an oil base at Awali, south of Muharraq, perhaps he came up from there. On one occasion he cornered me in the evening, plagueing me to direct him to Jim Connor's place. I couldn't help him, neither could anyone else for no one had heard of Jim Connor's place. Next day he told us that he had indeed found it. What he had failed to point out to us was that what he sought and indeed had found was the bar at the Gymkhana Club a very pleasant social cum sporting spot hence 'Jim Connor's' place.

Surprisingly, the catering at Bahrain was first class, being in the hands of an ex-Indian Army NCO known to all and sundry as the Major. A tall smart elegant figure with a bristling grey military moustache. For reasons never known to us he shuttled between Bahrain and Karachi over the years controlling the dining arrangements in the rest houses at both aviation centres. He ruled with a rod of iron and although he was not directly responsible for the cooking, his overall discipline and desire for efficiency, obviously rubbed off on to the kitchen *wallahs*. I recall this, and like conversations, 'Major, what the hell is wrong tonight, where's the food. I've been here well over five minutes already'. 'Sorry sahib, all my fault, my arse needs kicking, all coming right away' – and it did! Ah – the days of *Raj* – or were they?

Anyway, on this my first venture East in the mighty flying boat, we were awakened early on the morning of 26 March for a comparatively short, single sector flight, to Karachi. As always in the East, we were awoken with the mandatory cup of hot sweet tea, then a very substantial breakfast at the rest house before being transported ahead of our passengers to the marine base.

Having left the boat in a serviceable state, she had been refuelled and sat bobbing gently up and down in the clear waters just off the causeway. Even at this early hour, with the sun hardly more than a few degrees above the horizon, the heat was beginning to bear down, only serving to accentuate the high relative humidity of the air which must have approached 100 per cent.

A quick check of the prepared flight plan data and then on to the launch and on board as soon as possible. If one could get airborne before reaching total saturation, there was a reasonable chance of cooling off by allowing air to flow through the open cockpit side windows, although it was necessary to gain a few thousand feet in height before detecting any appreciable fall in temperature. There were even occasions when due to a fall in surface temperature at night, an inversion occurred causing temperature above the surface to be higher than that on the surface, so one just couldn't win sometimes.

Jaded passengers on board, engines started and following a quick word of command from No. 1, the radio officer slipped the mooring rope from off the bollard and forward we went. As at many of the coastal or lake marine bases there was an almost unlimited stretch of water, so once the launch crews had driven off any stray vessels, the throttles were opened and the giant hull started to move, almost reluctantly ahead over the clear water, with engines going flat out to produce power in the hot, moist salt-laden air. Later, rather than sooner, we came up on to the step and then a surge as the beast began to fight free of the water. A visible hearty yank on the control column and we came unstuck, to move rapidly forward, but hardly upward. One rarely climbed up and away in a fully laden flying boat and it was usually a long slow process with the rate of climb indicator showing a few hundred feet per minute. There were occasions when it was necessary to level off, cool off, and then gain speed and resume climbing again although this was hardly usual. The eastward flight out from Bahrain is over clear blue-green water dotted with numerous Arab vessels either engaged in fishing, transporting goods or even, I am told, pearl diving. The first few hundred miles follows this pattern, until thrusting ominously into the hazy sky ahead, can be seen the hills, or more properly called, the mountains, of the Oman or Sharjah peninsular which jut out from the Arabian mainland, almost to the Iranian coast. The narrow gap which remains between the two is known as the Straits of Hormuz.

All of the rocky desert territory to the south side of the Gulf at that time formed the Trucial States, most of the land coming under the control of the Sultan of Oman, I believe.

The western edge of the peninsular was relatively flat and mainly desert, with small river inlets where villages such as Sharjah and Abu Dhabi provided a haven for local fisherman. Such has been the development of oil exploration in these parts that they are now almost major cities, with high rise buildings, airports, roads and all major conveniences. They call that progress I believe.

The spine of the peninsular consists of rugged uninviting-looking mountains, over which, at certain times of the year, moist air could build up very quickly into high level thunderstorms, but whatever the conditions it was always satisfying to move out over the sea to the east and to be clear of that stark-looking mountain range.

Our track then closed with the south coast of Iran, which was equally wild and rugged. It varied from areas of yellow-brown sand with rock outcrops to an occasional dried up river bed or *wadi*, with miniature jagged mountains which came down almost to the sea. At the levels at which we flew, one could gain an impressive side view of some of these rocky areas and so harsh did some of these rock masses look that the veteran skippers had come to recognise them and had devised appropriate names for them. One for very obvious reason being known as the Manhattan Skyline.

Spaced at broad intervals along this coast were landing strips set up in the days when Imperial Airways flew the grand old Armstrong Whitworth Ensign aircraft through to India and these strips were still visible. This was comforting because they all bordered the water and so an emergency alighting alongside meant that at least some form of life would be found nearby. At the far end of the Hormuz Strait was the airstrip at Jāsk and still further along another at Gwadar whilst just over the border into Baluchistan, another strip remained at Jiwani. I once had occasion to be a member of a land plane crew which was forced to divert to Jiwani when Karachi was waterlogged – yes waterlogged – and the sole facilities at Jiwani were an old Imperial Airways hut, fuel from stored drums with no accommodation whatsoever, so we were obliged to sleep on the wing of the aircraft during our enforced stay. Recreation, yes certainly, the Shell Oil Company representative, provided us with a few .303 rifles and we spent the day jackal hunting. A far cry from package holidays wasn't it?

Again navigation was no problem since our track followed the west/east run of the Iranian and Baluchistan coasts until approaching Karachi, at which point a powerful radio beacon beckoned us in towards the city. The alighting area was to the south of the city at Korangi Creek where a marine base had been in existence for many years. It did possess limited accommodation but, in fact, on arrival we were transported to the city in rickety ex-service buses repainted in BOAC livery.

The journey into town was made mainly in the dark, there being nothing to see since it was almost a desert track anyway. The only signs of life were the camel trains heading for the coast to collect or deliver I know not what. These trains consisted of numerous camels, each pulling a flat topped two- or four-wheeled cart, all in line astern. The lead truck had a lantern perched aloft as did the last vehicle, but each camel seemed to fix its gaze on the one ahead almost like circus elephants nose to tail and the few drivers on board were all seemingly asleep. Certainly the lead man seemed to be.

It was at this stage that I was told a very amusing story concerning these camel trains, although I never saw such a thing happen myself. It was said that certain crew members had become past masters at diverting the camel trains whilst the far from zealous drivers were fast asleep. The crew transport would be halted whilst an 'expert' alighted and approaching the lead camel, with the driver far away in dreamland, he would gently turn the animal in a wide semi-circle, and head him back up the road in the opposite direction. Being a creature of habit and presumably used to the journey either way, this camel would then continue happily on ahead, back to the departure point, whilst the others, again from sheer habit, religiously followed their leader until the whole train was homeward bound again. I would have thought, if the story were true, that the drivers would have arranged for at least one of their number to be awake at all times to forestall this 'naughty' crew activity, but I gather that it continued for many months. Since these labourers were hardly famed for their energy and dedication to work, there was every reason to suppose that the prank was workable and hence did in fact occur.

The hotel accommodation in Karachi was hardly to be recommended to other travellers, but since our routes were in the process of development, one had to accept whatever came along and in any case our passengers had gone on with the aircraft on the next stage of their journey. This change was part of the so called 'slip crew' system whereby one crew took the flying boat and passengers over certain stages of the total journey and then at pre-arranged points one crew would step off whilst another would take over and fly the next sector or two. The time spent with a particular group of passengers and the night stop over at certain points varied very much until eventually the airline saw the wisdom of keeping the aircraft flying as long as possible. Incidentally this system did cut out passenger night stops, but increased the number of slip points at which crew changes took place. It also meant that taking a flight out of the United Kingdom for Singapore did not necessarily mean that this was your overseas destination and you could well finish up in Hong Kong or elsewhere.

As the route structure developed, we could study the somewhat complicated 'slip' graphs at our base and thereby trace the various sectors over which a particular crew would fly and more importantly establish the dates for return to Poole and home.

On this occasion we had the full day to wait in Karachi before the next flying boat came through and this enabled me to take a look at the variety of shops centred in Elphinstone Street. The 'in' purchases at that time, to be saved for the homeward flight, were one pound boxes of tea, good quality carpets of all sizes and gold or silver wire embroidery of a very high standard. Other activities took place involving bartering and the exchange of certain commodities. Many stories have been told, and indeed books written of the smuggling which followed these exchanges. I tell the truth when I say that my purchases were restricted to those, which although they sometimes stretched Customs allowances beyond reason, were not illegal in any other sense. In the years ahead a few crew members became very involved in the movement of gold and drugs and there are books available which recall how security staff traced and charged the culprits.

Like so many eastern cities, Karachi was a place of many contrasts. Poverty and riches, fine buildings and foul smells and the ever-present cattle wandering the streets whilst buzzards, or as they were affectionately known, 'Shite Hawks', circled lazily overhead looking for carrion and there was plenty of that.

Within a matter of hours, and in spite of taking sound advice with regard to food and alcohol, my stomach and rear end seemed full of hot coals and I could hardly move more than a few steps from the toilet. Being used to this kind of malady, the chief steward filled me up with a proprietary mixture including the old stand-by of kaolin and morphine and whatever else was pushed into these concoctions so that things settled down somewhat. Certainly by 'call time' on the day following I felt fully back in the land of the living.

The usual warm sweet tea came with the morning call and whilst subsequently taking breakfast, toast for me, we were informed that the incoming aircraft was on time and fully serviceable, so we boarded the crew transport and set off for Korangi in the morning twilight.

The boat was indeed on time and whilst passengers were offloaded for breakfast and it was refuelled, we went through the flight planning and other formalities for what was to be an eight hour flight to Calcutta, a quick transit stop and then another couple of hours or so on to Rangoon where we could roost for the night. Rangoon was not a 'slip stop', so our passengers would be spending the night there also.

The flight from Karachi to Calcutta covered, at one stage or another, every type of landscape to be seen across India although whether one saw it or not depended on the time of the year and the height flown.

During the North-east Monsoon season the weather could be delightful with clear skies, maybe a daily build-up of some cloud but plenty to be seen. One interesting feature of the effect of the North-east Monsoon over India, worthy of mention, is how it enabled other airborne creatures to unwittingly join us at our cruising altitude, which was normally around 8,000 feet. This phenomena was brought to my attention by one Captain who, as we cruised along about an hour out of Karachi, pointed to a black dot ahead and said, 'Watch that carefully'. At our speed, we quickly shot past the object which to my astonishment proved to be an enormous bird soaring quite unconcernedly in the clear air. A full explanation followed. Apparently the larger hawks or vultures, making full use of the thermal effects, just as happens with gliders, were uplifted many thousands of feet until the rising columns of warm air finally petered out, and there, as far as I could see, they stayed, gliding around quite effortlessly, until the heat of the day subsided.

The South-west Monsoon, however, was a far different story. In this day and age, large high-flying aeroplanes can climb up through the weather and generally sit on top. In the days of the flying boat you either flew in constant rain below cloud, in cloud or, if you were very lucky, between layers. Whatever happened it was grey, wet, hot and miserable and navigation, certainly by map-reading, was very difficult.

The climb out from Karachi was made over the Delta of the great River Indus and an area of what seemed to consist of endless water and mud flats known as the Rann of Kutch. Slipping in and out of cloud on the way up it was almost impossible to obtain a visual fix, as the pattern of rivulets, mud flats and water stretches never seemed to fit into any detail on our maps, certainly not on the maps which we carried in those days and so one had to wait for more prominent features later on in the flight which could then be clearly seen and identified. Taking the direct route meant that we passed north of Ahmadabad en route to Bhopal and thence to Calcutta.

I have already mentioned the South-west Monsoon, which brings rain to Karachi, but to the south, particularly in the Bombay region, the rainfall is far higher and across to the east and up from the Bay of Bengal into the Ganges Delta into what was Burma, the volume of rainfall has to be seen to be believed. In a normal year, the progress of the South-west Monsoon north eastwards is so predictable that the weathermen are able to draw position lines on the maps forecasting almost the precise day on which the monsoon should arrive at each point.

There is no point in boring a reader with the land features seen whilst crossing India, but having read numerous books, when I was a lad, describing this vast country, I was always intrigued and used to watch out for the old walled cities, many set up and ruled over by the *Rajas*.

During the South-west Monsoon, upper winds tended to be predominantly westerly, hence with the wind blowing behind us we could usually rely on a fairly fast crossing to Calcutta but of course coming back it was a vastly different story. Quite frequently, even with a full fuel load, it became necessary to pop in somewhere to seek a top up of fuel and there weren't many spots which could handle a large flying boat in the middle of India.

However, BOAC managed to find a lake, moved in their marine staff and set up a refuelling stop at, believe, Raj Samand. I have struggled to pinpoint this lake on modern maps but can't find it, although it must still exist since it was a holy lake bounded by a dam. I seem to recall that it was somewhere in the region of Udaipur, but that matters not.

I don't know how many BOAC flying boat veterans are still around but I'll wager that they all remember this lake, if only for the dam wall. I seem to recall a temple on a small island in the lake and we were told hair-raising stories of the number of locals who had been eaten by crocodiles said to inhabit the lake. All good stuff especially when you were sitting in a small crew launch on your way to or from your aircraft. On my first visit to this famed spot, the prevailing wind and available take-off run meant that we had no choice but to take off towards the high wall of the dam. If only I'd had a video camera in those days to record what was truly one of the most frightening experiences in my life. Flicking through the pages of my logbook I see that this occurred on the 30th of July 1947 whilst crewing a Hythe flying boat registered G-AGHK (*Harlequin*) under the command of Captain Pat White and it had taken us seven hours from Calcutta thus far to reach Raj Samand and seek more fuel. Crews delighted in relating amusing stories of their take-offs from Raj Samand but when you're sitting on board a mighty flying machine which starts moving slowly towards a massive wall on the commencement of a take-off run I can assure you that it is funny no longer. I well remember on this occasion, even when the flying boat was up on the step and moving really fast with speed continuing to build up, there seemed no way in which we were ever going to clear the high dam wall. Pat White was a cool customer and having yanked *Harlequin* off the water, he held her down until speed had built up and then with another hefty pull on the controls we shot up and over. It was far too close for my liking and I noticed that nobody had managed even the weakest of smiles thus far. Of course once over the top it was time for the experts to give forth. 'Close,! rubbish, when I was with old so and so, the coolies had to jump off the top we were so close.' Anyway I'll not forget this occasion and if you ever meet a flying boat man who flew the eastern routes ask him if he remembers Raj Samand and if he does, mention the dam wall and then stand back and listen.

The run in to Calcutta was well covered with prominent features such as rivers and large towns and so from the navigator's point of view, life was comparatively easy. Even if you were unfortunate enough to have a night crossing or arrive in fading light, the great iron and steelworks at Jamshedpur cast a brilliant yellow and golden light into the sky which could be seen for a great distance. A fine beacon to light the way on to Calcutta. In those early days, Calcutta was a transit stop and so as yet we had not been subjected to the filth and poverty of this huge city, added to which our alighting area was well to the north on the Hooghly River, and for those who know the Calcutta area, it was adjacent to the Great Willingdon Bridge. Here we were taken ashore with our passengers to primitive accommodation close by the Bridge and for many months this accommodation took the form of a houseboat. Here, whilst waiting for refuelling to take place we could sip cool lemonade and munch on doorstep sandwiches whilst watching the river traffic pass by. Mind you, if we had suffered a rough ride from Karachi few of us ate the locally-prepared food as there would undoubtedly be more rough weather to follow on the hop across the Bay of Bengal to Rangoon.

Huge freight barges, with teams of oarsmen, could be seen making their way up and down stream, but without the luxury of benches on which to sit, they stood in large groups sometimes facing aft and walked with the oars trailed to subsequently plunge them into the water like trained university boat crews and then reverse their movement pulling on the dipped oars as they did so. Often the process would be reversed as they pushed rather than pulled on the oars and all this was done to the accompaniment of some weird eastern chant as they worked away. Meanwhile further in towards the river bank could be seen sights which hardly tended to aid the appetite or digestion. Ablutions at the water's edge interrupted every now and then as the bloated bodies of a dead cow or some other creature drifting by, usually with one or more crows or buzzards perched on top, pulling away at the carcass. It is a dreadful thought that this scene went on all day every day.

With the OK from the launch crew and flight planning completed, it was out to the boat once again. Many stories centre on the take-off run at Calcutta also, although I was fortunate enough not to have experienced the favourite tale.

In high temperatures, aircraft performance was always down and so it was that, having moved up river to then turn and face the south and commence a take-off run, pilots were often faced with a loss of 'urge' from the engines. Approaching the Willingdon Bridge with no sign of coming on to the step, or gaining the necessary lift, the procedure should have been to abort the take-off run and start again. However one or two of the commmanders, faced with this problem, and being almost on the point of leaving the water, were reluctant to abandon take-off. What then? Well the answer was apparently simple, keep full power on, aim straight ahead, and under one of the bridge spans into open water on the far side, and then up, up and away, you hoped.

I couldn't argue the sense or the validity of these hair-raising procedures, but we never lost a boat by this process and many flight crews around at that time assured me that this sort of incident had happened to them. Flying produces enough hair-raising incidents without adding to them, so I guess I was lucky to have suffered one less.

I think that the short sector from Calcutta to Rangoon during the monsoon season, was one of the worst it was possible to endure. One would frequently leave Calcutta, heading in a south-easterly direction, probably in moderate rain but with grey, black or even brown clouds ahead warning of rough weather to come. We rarely attempted to climb up into the weather because you never knew what heavy storm clouds lay embedded in the general murk, and there was no way that you could climb over the top. Even today's jets sometimes have a problem doing just that, so we tended to stay below cloud, flying in the rain, with side windows open to obtain what little air we could.

Tracking out over the Ganges Delta, one saw nothing but river and mud flats and map-reading was virtually impossible. Invariably, once out over the Bay of Bengal the sky darkened and one entered the nearest thing to flying in solid water that could be imagined. Hot blinding rain, virtually one hundred per cent humidity, turbulence when least expected, and no radio contact at all, that being drowned out by static electricity. All that one could do was to drop down lower and lower often to a few hundred feet above sea level. No problems with high ground, since we knew that for an hour or more at least there was nothing but water, until we closed with the Arakan coast somewhere in the region south of Akyab at Ramree Island. It was all terribly depressing, and quite often the navigator and engineer officer would stand behind the pilots' seats joining them in their look out for some sort of weather clearance.

Maybe, if you were lucky, the sky above would brighten up a little and a gap or two appear. With fingers crossed, the aircraft would be eased up to a reasonable height in the hope that the cloud was indeed breaking and that the cloud base itself would be lifting. In truth it rarely did, and very soon the sky would darken once more, rain thundering against the windscreen and hull and it was then nose down and back to sea level yet again.

The closer one came to the Arakan coast, the more dangerous this tactic became, because the land was far from flat in that region. Fortunately we had been equipped with a fairly primitive form of radar which, transmitting and receiving on the same radio frequency, produced a fairly substantial blip on the radar screen once the coastline ahead gave a good return signal.

During the peak of the monsoon season, one could assume that whilst the weather was usually appalling on the western side of Burma and the Malay Peninsular, on the eastern side, an improvement was almost guaranteed, likewise the further south one moved so things improved also.

I don't think I ever failed to see the Arakan coast, since improving weather coupled with our primitive radar meant that one knew where to look when Mother Nature made it possible to see ahead. That is not to say that the weather always improved as you crossed Burma, it was just marginally better, although as one closed with Rangoon one had to be extremely unlucky not to pick up the vast Irrawaddy Delta and the large stretch of river which ran from Rangoon down to the Gulf of Martaban. In winter during the fine weather the finest landmark, visible from way off, was the sun reflecting off the great Golden Pagoda of Shwe Dagon.

At Rangoon, our alighting area was on the river opposite the city, amongst the large freighters anchored offshore, from whence we taxied gently into moorings close by the BOAC jetty.

Rangoon was a night stop, before the run down to Singapore on the next day and together with our passengers we were accommodated at the one-time famous Strand Hotel. Very similar, as I found out later, to many in India, particularly in Calcutta. The woodwork in the hotel lounges and bedrooms was mainly fine teak and this included the bulk of the furniture as well as fittings. One's every need was taken care of by the ever-present well-dressed 'bearers'. Food was, as one might expect in those early post-war days, pretty rough, but the beer was of passable quality, so all was well.

Our evening was spent in bargaining for beautifully carved teak elephants or other ornaments and teasing the purveyors of suspect rubies. With no knowledge of precious stones we tended to fight shy of any purchases, but I was told many years later that most of the stones available at that time were genuine and extremely good value for money. Nearly fifty years on, I still possess my teak elephant book-ends which look remarkably fine after a good polish.

In spite of the standard of accommodation, quality of food and the high temperatures and humidity, most of us awoke refreshed, partly due I guess to the fairly strenuous stretch of flying which we had undergone on the previous day. A few passengers and the odd crew member were disturbed by the huge creaking fans mounted in the ceiling which did their best to circulate the hot sticky air. Choice was limited, either put up with the noise of the fan, or switch it off and swelter throughout the night. Certainly it took time to become accustomed to these relics of past ages, but fatigue plus a beer or two provided the ultimate solution.

Anyway, another crack of dawn departure, except that it was difficult to determine dawn, the sky being overcast with rain falling steadily. A typical Rangoon departure for most of the year. Take off presented no problem as there was plenty of water and, having headed the great beast along the line of moored freighters, throttles were pushed forward and we ploughed slowly ahead through the murky water until that first surge forward indicated that we were on the step and away.

Our track to Singapore was predominantly southerly, to use a hackneyed nautical phrase, with a touch of east. There were no immediate prospects of a clear run south and we were resigned to another low-level soaking, although the weather forecast had indicated a slow break-up of cloud as the flight progressed. Apart from the normal monsoon weather we also had to contend with a band of thunderstorm-type weather called the Inter-Tropical Front, known today as the Inter-Tropical Convergence Zone. This line of weather normally occurred when two air masses of differing characteristics met and it tended to move north and south following, but lagging behind, the yearly latitude changes of the sun.

Weather forecasts tended to be standard in form and more

47

seasonal than daily. Veteran crews usually collected the data as a matter of routine, but had preconceived ideas about what lay ahead on most sectors at given times of the year.

The weather would undoubtedly break towards the south and would tend to be better on the eastern side of the Malay Peninsular. It was too dangerous to cross the Peninsular in cloud, for even when well above safety height and clear of any high ground we never knew what vicious storm clouds lay embedded in the other cloud. This of course was long before the advent of weather radar, which now makes it possible to pick up and display such weather on the flight deck equipment. I recall that, true to form, the sky did lighten and brighten and the odd blue patch appeared well above until finally, in the region of the Mergui Archipelago, it opened up into well broken, but rapidly developing white cumulus cloud.

Such were the hot vertical air currents in this part of the world, one could clearly watch the heavy lumps of cotton wool rising and expanding at one and the same time. The wily old captains never fell into the trap of heading for seemingly clear spots in the hope of surmounting a cloud top, or flying through a clear gap between two clouds.

Many times I have sat in an aircraft, with a not so experienced pilot, with engines running flat out, climbing and heading for a gap in the clouds with the intention of pushing out into the clear air on the far side, only to find that as the aircraft climbed, so the cloud built up at a faster rate and more importantly expanded to close the gap. On more than one occasion the aircraft was headed into such a gap, just as it closed, and it was then that the 'forces of nature' came to be fully appreciated.

Turbulence was violent, to the extent that pilots could be seen fighting the controls with the aircraft instruments shuddering throughout the manoeuvre, particularly the air speed indicator and altimeter which fluctuated in a crazy fashion. Until indoctrinated, there was a tendency to suspect that such a massive and heavy flying machine could hardly ride out this type of weather. Thankfully it could, since the Sunderland and its civil variants were built like battleships, although that did not prevent nature in the form of violent vertical currents of air proving just how powerful she was and thereby earning our respect. The developing cumulus type cloud, triggered off by the high ground on the Peninsular, was already pushing higher and higher and obviously beginning to form the dreaded cumulo-nimbus storm cloud. This would, during

48

the course of the day pour down buckets of rain usually, as far as Singapore was concerned, around 4 p.m. on a regular basis.

Anyway it was obviously preferable to stay to the west and mainly along the coast until reaching Phuket point, and then on a slightly more south-easterly heading, down past Penang, Kuala Lumpur and Malacca and on to Singapore.

The ground features changed slowly as we moved south and I found it quite fascinating to see the long stretches of clear deserted sandy beaches, palm fringed, and then to looked further inland to see the darker green of what I took to be rubber or the dreaded jungle. It is interesting to note that Phuket, then a deserted and seemingly idyllic spot, is now a very popular holiday resort for those who like to travel further afield than Europe.

Along the Straits of Malacca, I was quite surprised at the volume of sea traffic involving merchant vessels of all sizes but I guess that this was symptomatic of an area which was struggling to come alive again.

The famed Johore Causeway to our left and Singapore ahead, we sought out the alighting area which was in the open sea, riddled with moored vessels, Rangoon style, but worse.

The problem with alighting at Singapore was that quite often there was broad swell, with the wind at right angles to the direction of the swell. This could be treacherous in the closing stages of a final approach into wind, particularly if one clipped a peak or landed in a trough of the swell. The precise technicalities escape me, but I do recall a bounce on one such occasion, followed by a resounding crash, which convinced me once and for all that such conditions of sea and wind could be very frightening unless dealt with by an expert, and certainly the outcome could sometimes ensure easy bowel movement.

Ted Brand was a skilled man and coped well with the moderate swell that day, and we then ploughed through the water following the launch into the inner harbour, or lake as it seemed to me, of Kallang, right alongside one part of the city.

An easy mooring, quick pick up for passengers and crew and we were transported through a seedy part of the old town eastwards along the coast to the well known Seaview Hotel.

Seaview was not quite in the style of the famed Raffles Hotel, but it was extremely comfortable as far as BOAC crews were concerned. Almost on the seashore, it was but a short distance to the swimming club, and in the years ahead, I spent many happy hours there in the company of good companions. That evening, after dinner, the crew decided to adjourn to what I was told was Mooi Heng's nightclub (I hope I have the spelling right). With visions of soft lights, sweet music and exotic eastern belles, I followed the mob across the road to Heng's. Mooi Heng was a wrinkled old Chinaman who ran a general store in a tin and palm-roofed shack, close enough to the Seaview Hotel to ensure a safe and speedy return to base if one over-indulged.

There we sat on upturned crates and drank endless bottles of Tiger beer at a fraction of the hotel price, whilst I listened to some of the old sweats relate stories of flying boat incidents and accidents which were enough to give me cause to think of resignation and a boat trip home.

What wonderful days these were, and to my mind they were really a continuation of the friendly atmosphere and *esprit de corps* which I thought I had left behind in the RAF. I guess, since the bulk of the BOAC air crews were ex-RAF, this wonderful atmosphere, on and off duty, was fully understandable.

Some mellow, some full of song and some just plain drunk, our party eventually recrossed the road back to Seaview and to a well-earned rest.

The following day commenced with a superb breakfast, leading off with fresh pineapple and a compote of tropical fruits and then a traditional English breakfast, even down to the sausages. All this whilst small birds circled the domed roof of the dining room, some of the more adventurous sparrows and finches coming down and landing on the breakfast table to seek out scraps.

As a new boy, my day had been programmed by the others, starting with a visit to the city before the sun pushed temperatures too high for comfort. A number of us piled into a ramshackle old taxi and off we went. The road back to town passed through some of the seedier sections, although even they could not match the squalor of parts of Indian cities. The driver tried to coax some of us into a funfair, named 'Happy World' I believe, but since the suggestion came from such a villainous looking creature it was totally ignored.

I recall that most of my time was taken up with shopping and although the large stores had almost everything imaginable on display, my purchases were all carried out in the notorious 'Change Alley'. You could buy almost anything here from cameras and binoculars down to lighters, most of them carrying well known brand names and most of them being fakes. However, the quality seemed to be pretty good and I think that I had moderate success in the bargaining battles, so I came away satisfied.

We assembled at an appointed time and then made our way to the sports and swimming club, part way along the road back to Seaview. On this day as on most free days over the years thereafter, I was content to spend all my time at this haven of rest. After all the suffering and damage in this part of the world, the club was now back to what I assumed to be its pre-war status and appearance. Whatever our needs they were provided for here, although most of our time was spent lounging on the grass area adjacent to the pool, or sipping cool beer at the bar. Almost as if by routine, the sky to the south then began to darken as the cumulus clouds, which had slowly been developing all day, demonstrated that they had now developed into storm clouds, and were about to open up and deposit buckets of visible moisture upon us. So speedily back to Seaview, a wash, change and crew assembly for dinner. What a life, and presumably it was a part taste of pre-war conditions in these far eastern colonies.

After dinner, I was introduced to the game of 'Liar Dice' which occupied most of our time until a very late hour, although conscious of the fact that we had an early start next day, the boss knew when to blow the whistle. Incidentally I purchased my own set of poker dice after that trip, and never travelled without them, indeed they still sit in the side pocket of my suitcase, a hedge against future boredom.

Our 'take-over' flying boat, G-AGHK (*Harlequin*) had now arrived safely from Calcutta and was handed over to us by the incoming crew. During that afternoon we were informed that it was fully serviceable and ready for the morrow.

After yet another pre-dawn call and a breakfast with morning twilight just showing in the east, we were off to the marine base at Kallang to join the waiting launch, where a station officer had prepared our flight plan which I was able to check very rapidly, since our next sector was in no way critical as far as time and fuel were concerned.

Fortunately the sea was moderately calm and having boarded our passengers, we moved slowly out of the harbour into open sea, whilst base launches directed us to the take-off area. The usual exhilarating build-up of noise, spray and speed followed and then we were up and away with a quick turn to port (left) and across the island, passing over the notorious Changi

51

area, now an airfield once again, and the RAF marine base at Seletar.

Even at this early hour, cloud could be seen building up over the Malay Peninsular, but as we were now heading for Bangkok, we could stay to the east of any high ground or cloud build-up, although residual storms from the previous evening could be seen sitting out over the sea ahead, sufficiently well dispersed so as to be easily avoidable.

This was not to be a particularly arduous flight since it would take about five and a half hours, and proved to be quite pleasant when compared with the flight down over the Bay of Bengal forty-eight hours earlier.

Mainly bright sunlit sea and sky with about half cumulus cloud cover, which as yet had not started to build up. So it was on and up to Bangkok, where our alighting area was on the river although precisely where depended very much on prevailing wind conditions since the river had numerous bends and stretches. There was always a suitable spot where one could alight, making absolutely certain that you were directly into the wind.

We were lucky on this occasion and were able to set down just alongside the mooring position by the Customs shed. On a later occasion, I recall a hilarious outcome, after being forced to land several miles up river due to the wind direction. The skipper having finished the landing run, turned around and headed back the few miles to the marine base. However, becoming tired of ploughing along at a slow rate through the murky river, he reopened the throttles and gradually as speed increased, brought the flying boat up on to the step. I stood looking out of the Perspex astrodome, almost in hysterics at the outcome. The aircraft had in fact now effectively become a giant high speed launch with a massive churning wake trailing behind. From the skipper's point of view it was great fun hurling this almost airborne monster along the centre of the wide river, but for the poor locals in their sampans it almost spelled disaster. I watched as the backwash picked up one after another raising it as if to hurl it on to the river bank only for the poor little vessel to fall back into the trough and be drawn back into the river again as we passed by. They must have been furious but surprisingly I never heard any mention of complaint to, or at, the base. Perhaps they thought it was fun too, although I doubt it.

It was but a short ride into the city where we were accommodated at one of the few first-class hotels to exist in those early post-war days.

I stopped over in Bangkok on many occasions in the years which followed but I always remained fascinated by its beauty and the friendliness of its people. I know in modern times it has become regarded as a city of sin and degeneracy, but I suspect that the changes which have taken place are simply in response to the demands of westerners who seek solace in the atmosphere of this great city. For my part I have always regarded Bangkok as one of the cleanest and most enjoyable stopover points in the late forties. Mind you the same relationship between east and west still prevailed in those days and there was plenty to see and do to titillate the eyes and minds of aircrews, as yet unaccustomed to the unbelievable and uninhibited behaviour of the locals.

One spot in Bangkok much favoured by lusty young crew members was part of a local Chinese theatre, titled I believe the Bam Bin Boon. On my first conducted visit to this place I found that one entered via a local market, where in small side stalls and huts, coolies, for want of a better description, could be seen stretched out in cots, eyes glazed, bodies sweating, gently pulling on what we assumed were opium pipes. They were quite oblivious to our presence and we to theirs, for we had other things on our minds, but the sweet stench was overpowering. The first time I entered the theatre I was somewhat bemused to see a Chinese costume drama taking place on the stage, to the accompaniment of shrill voices and the sound of massive gongs and cymbals crashing every few seconds. I couldn't imagine why we had been taken to such a spot, but all became clear very shortly afterwards. Proceeding up through the body of the theatre we were led to a low balcony at the rear where there was a small curtained stage. Having ensured that we were all comfortably seated, our 'host' who couldn't speak a word of English, gave a word of command when to the accompaniment of what I again assumed to be Chinese music, about a dozen almost naked young girls entered. Almost naked because each wore a clear square plastic panel, suspended by a waist cord, to conceal their naughty bits. They did little more than parade around the stage, attempting to synchronise their movements to music and then at a given signal they all came forward and lined up along the front of the stage, the atmosphere being almost like the war-time shows at the Windmill Theatre in London, in that the regulars and veterans commandeered the front rows in anticipation of the next stage in the programme.

I must confess that what followed left me cold, as the locals would place a few banknotes at the feet of the chosen lady and she in turn would lift the plastic flap for her admirer to see what had thus far been left to the imagination. Then almost as if on the press of a button, down went the flap and it was all over. What a life.

Fortunately for us one of the ground staff ladies, who was around ninetieth in the line of succession to the royal throne, had her own accommodation in one of the palace compounds. Many times she invited crew members to dine with her and this was an eye opener when one saw the somewhat primitive gap between royal family and servants, since at that time immediately on crossing the threshold, servants went down on to their knees and crawled forward with heads bowed. All very embarrassing for us as guests, but obviously accepted as part and parcel of their lives. As best I can recall, our hostess's name was Nundha Phung Bun, a charming lady, who at one time trained as a nurse in London and spoke almost perfect English. Apart from the pleasure of visiting her 'at home', she was able to organise local transport and guides enabling us to view the beautiful temples which abound in and around the city.

I remember also that the Shell Oil Company representative, who obviously had close links with the airline, frequently arranged outings for us too. The most enjoyable and most frequently sought after was to the Mekong brewery. They produced a local beer named after the great river which flows through that part of the world. For some unknown reason we were not permitted to visit the distillery which went under the same name, but I think maybe that had something to do with the formula in use which rumour had it led to many recorded cases of blindness after over-indulgence. Maybe they were using the river water in its manufacture since the river Mekong hardly runs with the clarity of a Scottish brook. However, discussion on the subject was denied and we were certainly barred from entry.

Our initial stay in Bangkok came to an end far too soon, but I confess to a certain keenness to move on as our next port of call was the Crown Colony of Hong Kong.

Flying boats were the first choice of air transport for this colony as post-war development had not yet got underway and the only airfield was a small strip at Kai Tak positioned roughly where today's modern airport is sited but in a far more dangerous position in those days. The approach for a landplane was normally from the west almost entirely over the built up area of Kowloon, with a last minute dive on to the extremely short runway, at the end of which was a hill with a small gap to one side. All very frightening.

This of course meant that take-off by landplanes had to be towards the east, with high ground ahead immediately after take-off unless one was prepared for a death-defying violent right-hand turn immediately on becoming airborne.

Anyway this was no concern of ours, since we had the whole harbour area upon which to alight, and even then there were still many alternatives if that area was not available.

The period during which we flew this route was long before the Vietnamese war, when the land between Bangkok and Hong Kong was part Siam and part Cochin China and one could fly in a direct line from Bangkok to Hong Kong without any risk of being shot at. This was completely new territory to me and I was fascinated after take-off from Bangkok as we climbed away to the north-east, at the brilliant green carpet which lay below, jungle or swamp I knew not, but the whole vista was most pleasing to the eye. Maps were still pretty inaccurate and the rivers and roads, what few there were, seemed to occur in the wrong places and were always the wrong shapes, until eventually the great broad sweep of the mighty Mekong river could be seen ahead. Little cloud and bright sun, so no problem obtaining a good visual fix, as we passed over the river, with the promise of a further reliable check whilst crossing the coast ahead, to the north of Hue.

So it was on until reaching the coast and then the great expanse of the Gulf of Tonkin lay ahead. In those days, BOAC had a couple of route alternative alighting areas, one at Haiphong on the mainland of Vietnam and another on the Chinese held island of Hainan.

These were extremely useful boltholes, particularly when in the spring and autumn, Hong Kong could quickly close in with low cloud, drizzle and fog although as I will explain later, one advantage of the flying boat was that, in certain circumstances, it was possible to come down in the sea, well away from the formal alighting area, and then taxy in. This was a long and arduous procedure but at least it ensured a safe arrival at one's destination. In addition, on this first journey up to Hong Kong, I now heard talk of a phenomenon as yet unknown to me, the typhoon, which frequently came roaring up from the Gulf to affect the whole of the Chinese mainland. The colony was, of course, quite accustomed to dealing with the problem of high winds and the tides which resulted from typhoons, and as regular visitors will know even in those days, there were properly constructed typhoon shelters for small craft.

From our point of view as aviators, we often managed to get in and out before or after the worst of these storms, but if this was not possible, then the flight would be delayed, or perhaps diverted if necessary to an alternative. It wasn't too bad, as far as flying boats were concerned, because after the services were reopened, the Chinese gave sanction for BOAC to use the harbour, just northwards along the coast, at the old port of Swatow.

I well recall being aboard the first flying boat to visit this port, with a view to assessing its suitability as a diversion site. I was astounded at the hundreds of craft plying to and fro in the huge bay and there seemed no way in which we could ever find a clear run for landing. However, having established contact with one of our own launches which had been transported up to Swatow for the occasion, we were astonished to discover how quickly the alighting area could be cleared.

After an uneventful landing, the secret was revealed. Chinese military launches with crews out to create a good impression, simply fired at all and sundry showing signs of entering or crossing the alighting zone. We noticed this particularly as we moved out for our take-off run, when these vessels again beat up everything in sight until all was clear. It certainly proved to be a good alternative alighting area, but I cannot recall it ever being used after our visit.

Hong Kong consists of the main island, with a group of outlying islands and a section of the Chinese mainland known as the New Territories. The capital, Victoria, is on the north side of the main island, facing Kowloon in the New Territories, across the water. This expanse of sea provided the main anchorage for large vessels and a passageway for all other traffic. Ferries ploughed across the harbour areas between these two centres, all day every day. In the late forties trade and industry were just beginning to gear up but the high rise office blocks of today had not even started to appear: indeed on the Kowloon side, a hotel used by BOAC crews, the dear old Peninsular, was probably one of the highest buildings in existence. Today, I am told, it is dwarfed by the host of surrounding modern developments.

I won't dwell upon the delights of Hong Kong, for they were many and catered for all tastes. Suffice it to say that shoppers could spend hours and a small fortune in the radio, watch and souvenir shops along the famed Nathan Road and there was cheap drink and tobacco aplenty for those who so required.

There were many opportunities for amusement, apart from the

obvious ones, during our many stopovers in the Crown Colony. Just four, to give you the flavour!

The construction of the Peninsular Hotel was such that the main block formed the shape of a letter H, hence rooms on one side had a direct view into those opposite.

I recall, on one occasion, that our group of crew members congregating in one room for a post-flight beer spotted the Captain in a room across the way, emerging naked from his shower into the bedroom.

Quick as a flash, the co-pilot picked up a telephone and dialling the Captain's room, followed up in a very solemn voice with the statement that the caller was the Bishop of Hong Kong and had been disgusted at what he had seen whilst glancing idly from his bedroom window, furthermore it was his intention to take up this matter of gross indecency with the authorities.

How the skipper couldn't hear our laughter defeats me, as we were practically hysterical at his efforts to handle the phone, and conceal his naughty bits at the same time. The sequel matters not, but thank goodness we were all blessed with a reasonable sense of humour in those days.

Another pastime was 'coolie bombardment'. The crescent-shaped road at the hotel entrance was always packed with rickshaws and their drivers, all lined up, taxi style, awaiting business. As the evening wore on and service calls declined, the coolies would climb into their rickshaws and doze off. At this stage, participants would commence inflating locally made condoms with water to provide missiles. Not too much water in case the missile burst, yet not too little, lest the missile should become aerodynamically unstable in flight. Then, all hands to the window and combining Newton's Law of gravity, with what may be Boyle's Law on expansion, the missile was thrown at the correct angle for a strike. Not too vertical in case it struck the canopy over the hotel entrance, yet not too far forward in case it burst under inertia. A good strike did no harm, but it certainly produced an outburst of garbled 'Cantonese', or whatever, and in any event the coolies soon became wise, and pulled their rickshaw canopies forward for protection.

The crew accommodation in the Peninsular Hotel was on the top floor, where a one-time ballroom had been partitioned off to form a number of rooms, all surmounted by a kind of dropped false ceiling. At that time there were undeniable amorous links between male and female crew members, but any form of close activity tended to be limited as it was said that the room boys would pad about above the false ceiling in an attempt to view love-making activities through ceiling vents.

This it was said, precluded normal contact and led to assignations in the en suite toilet and bathrooms and on one occasion, since the bed was supposedly visible from above, by conducting the said activity, under the bed. Oh, what fun and mummy never knew.

I can also recall an occasion when an over-zealous steward departed one evening to meet the wife of a local Chinese worker, and comfort her during his absence on duty. Our friend failed to return that night and it was well into the next day before he did so and when he did, what a sight.

Apparently, whilst he was comforting the lady, her husband returned unexpectedly and our friend was bundled unceremoniously into the garden, by the wife and told to hide in the chicken shed. This he did, but apparently when he tried to slip off, the garden was surrounded by an unsurmountable wall and in any event the chickens kicked up one heck of a din when he attempted to move. The upshot was that he was forced to spend the night with the chickens, until hubbie moved off next day. His appearance on return was bad enough, but the stench from his clothing was unbearable. There has to be a moral to this story somewhere. I suppose it is that if you must have an affair with another man's wife, kill his chickens first.

Our handling agent in the colony was that great Far Eastern company Jardine Mathieson, who were, and I am told still probably are, 'Hong Kong'. They were regarded almost as the founders of the colony and the stories of alleged trade practices in far off days can hardly be repeated.

Our approach to Hong Kong was usually towards the south-eastern tip of the main island, thence to take up a northerly heading for Waglan Island, where, if all went well one could make a smart left turn, through the gap between island and mainland and into the main bay area for alighting.

This was all well and good in fine weather but when the seasonal low cloud and mist took over it could all become rather hazardous. To assist in the approach a primitive radar beacon had been positioned near to the south-eastern approach area, and the cliffs on the mainland shore had been broken to provide a Dover style white cliffs effect for ready identification.

So, in bad weather, it was usually a question of a slow descent to below cloud, heading for the eastern approach point, often in heavy rain or drizzle, but with a reassuring blip on our radar screen signifying that the beacon lay ahead, at the same time indicating its range.

It was then usually a case of all eyes peering ahead through the grey murk, looking for the white cliffs and if I recall correctly a lighthouse perched on Waglan Island. Mark you, we never engaged in such an approach unless we had already received an assurance that the cloud base and visibility were somewhat better in the bay area. That being so, as soon as the cliffs appeared ahead, it was usually possible to see the approach gap to the left and the harbour beyond. So it was then a case of a smart banking turn to the left and in towards the alighting area.

CHAPTER 4

SETTLING INTO ROUTINE

For the next year or so, with stand off periods of up to four weeks between overseas trips, which themselves lasted for up to twenty-eight days, I spent many happy hours in flight and on the ground at stopover points, and I shall always remember those days as some of the most enjoyable of my long aviation career. On the subject of time away from home, the effect was very ably summed up by one of our veteran stewards who, with a dead pan expression on his face, said ... 'Hope the wife isn't in the bath when I get home, these uniforms are a brute to get dry'. One came to know the routes remarkably well and since we were not flying at the great heights used by today's aircraft, there were many ground features which, weather permitting, became so familiar that maps were not always necessary.

Amongst the many characters who commanded these great flying boats was one 'Tich' Staples, who having settled his five feet four inch frame on to his well padded cushion in the left hand seat, since he could hardly see out without, would open up a school atlas and once away he would invariably call out visual checkpoints long before the poor old navigator had time to sort things out for himself. Most frustrating but in many ways still helpful.

The Hythe had a pretty good record for serviceability but there were occasions when, for one reason or another, an engine had to be shut down followed usually by a return to the departure point. Although these aircraft could fly comfortably on three engines, the loss of an engine still led to quite a reduction in speed, which did not help when one was anxious to get back on to safe water again as soon as possible.

On one occasion in the summer of 1947 whilst on our way east from Basra we had the misfortune to have both port engines malfunction, with a need to shut them down. This was disconcerting to say the least, and we were a much relieved crew when G-AGHW (*Hamilton*), was thumped somewhat unceremoniously down on to the Shatt al Arab river. Our passengers were eventually taken on by a replacement crew and aircraft, and we then spent nine days in the sweltering heat of Iraq, while both engines were changed using a pontoon floated out to our moorings. It was obviously a monumental task since there were no beaching facilities and daytime temperatures reached 100 degrees Fahrenheit, plus.

We were fortunate in a way because the Port Club at Basra granted us temporary membership and with all the facilities set up by the long serving Brits employed by the oil companies and port authorities, we found the swimming pool and catering services adequate compensation for our unwelcome delay, although nothing could take away the heat. No air conditioning in those days – just those dreadful gigantic fans set high in the ceilings and grinding away day and night like airborne concrete mixers.

Once the engine change had been completed and a satisfactory flight test carried out, we flew the empty aircraft home. Incidentally, during our enforced stopover we were offered rather primitive fishing gear and whilst none of us was sufficiently enthusiastic to use it, we did watch the locals engage in a spot of angling and I was astounded to see someone pull a shark out of the river, just downstream from our mooring. Not a large one, but a shark nonetheless.

In the months which followed our abortive trip, two newer types of flying boat were to arrive at our base. Both were basically Sunderland aircraft, but now these sleek ships looked very much civil aircraft and less like the Coastal Command giants to which the Hythe was so closely related.

The first to arrive was the *Plymouth*, powered by Pratt & Whitney Twin Wasp engines, and all of these machines were christened with names commencing with the letter 'P', *Pembroke, Portsea, Portsmouth, Perth* etc. These were followed by the more sophisticated Solent, powered by Bristol Hercules engines and logically named, *Stornoway, Scarborough, Severn* etc. Finally we received yet another version called the Sandringham, one of which, as a sole survivor of those days, was recently refurbished and flown off from the United Kingdom to Ireland I believe. Fortunately for me, the arrival of the Solent meant a change of route, for although they were not used exclusively on any particular route there was a tendency to use them on the run down through Central Africa to Johannesburg. It may well have been that the Hercules engines performed better in the higher take-off altitudes on that route as on occasions we operated out of water at 4-5,000 feet above sea level.

It is worth referring to the African route in some detail since in the period which followed the change of route, I met many of the old 'characters' from Imperial Airways or veteran Coastal Command skippers, all of whom were now almost as African as the route itself. Coupled with this there was much more of interest to be seen particularly when, as there was no need for cruising at vast altitudes, we could take our passengers almost to surface level, when there was something worth seeing below.

Incidentally, there was a feature of the flying boat which caused much amusement and attention but which, now that I am older and hopefully wiser, I must accept, produced unforgivable behaviour. To the rear of the lower deck, aft of the various compartments there was a small observation lounge where passengers could stand and chat if they wished. From this area, a small set of steps ran up and forward into an upper compartment containing beds or bunks.

This was of no great significance to me, until on one occasion, when we had picked up a party of attractive young ladies, listed as mannequins, they decided to use this compartment as a changing room. Working away at my allotted task in flight, I became aware that the first officer and I were the only ones actively engaged in work on the flight deck. No captain, radio officer, or engineer. Looking back I saw all three of them crouched against the rear flight deck compartment bulkhead with their backs towards me. 'Why don't you go and join them,' said the first officer and interest now aroused, I did so.

Between the crew compartment and the rest compartment was a metal door, used for emergency purposes, and as yet unknown to me, this was punctured with a number of rivet holes, which when the eye was applied to them, with difficulty, revealed all beyond. I suppose if one individual had been caught in the act, he would have felt guilty but as four persons were now totally engaged in this dubious activity, it was regarded as a joke even if the grins were somewhat sheepish. Dirty little boys!

I suppose if those young ladies are around today, they are in the 70s and they would doubtless forgive us our sins, or indiscretions, whichever you choose. I must confess that the visible beauties which lay beyond that door certainly stirred our young hearts a trifle.

My first adventure south into Africa started in mid-June of 1948 with a trip to Johannesburg. The existing crew rostering system meant that it would take us four days to reach our outward destination and certainly the first two days were extremely hard work. Not for us a comfortable night stop at Augusta, for since we now had the Solent, the increased speed and range meant that crews could be used more economically by extending their working day.

Thus it was that we flew for six and a half hours from Southampton to Augusta, spent an hour refuelling and then four and a half hours on to Cairo for a well-earned night stop. Incidentally, the aircraft did not carry on with another crew from Cairo as the slip crew system had not yet become operative on this route.

It was certainly new territory for me when early on the following morning we started our flight south from Cairo, roughly following the Nile to Khartoum. How bleak and uninviting the area looked with nothing of interest other than the sight of the great river as it carved its way through brown and yellow desert below. Later on, indeed some months later, we were to use Luxor as a night stop but for the present it was simply a question of heading south with increasing turbulence as the sun got to work on the sand, producing a wild mix of up and down draughts which hardly helped us to digest the early morning eggs and bacon, and certainly tested the wing structure of the giant Short Brothers aircraft. Historically, Khartoum is, I am sure, a very interesting city, but for us it was just a hot dry dusty spot to be transitted as quickly as possible. The alighting area was on the White Nile some miles south of the city below the confluence of the White and Blue Niles, at a spot known as Gordon's Tree. The name of course made sense because of its links with that great General but the precise reason for this name I was never to learn. There was usually a period of about one hour whilst the refuelling barge and crew did their work, during which time cool drinks were provided under noisy unstable roof fans, whilst the navigator calculated his flight plan for the next sector which followed the White Nile back down to its source at Lake Victoria.

The changes in scenery on this next five and a half hour leg were quite remarkable, ranging from harsh dry sand in the north to the rich green parkland bordering the north shore of the great lake.

Fortunately for me, on the occasion of my first Central African flight, the Captain was one of the flying boat veterans who was chock full of historical and geographical knowledge, all of which he imparted to the passengers at regular intervals.

After a slow climb out in the midday heat, we settled down to a moderately bumpy ride south towards our first checkpoint, the town of Malakal which sits on the Nile a little short of the point where the great river makes a temporary turn towards the west before heading south again to Juba.

There really was little of interest down below until well past Malakal although from a navigational point of view the clear line of the river provided useful checks on our progress. Between Malakal and Juba lie the great marshes of the Nile known as the Sudd, where the change to green becomes very marked. As we approached this area, the skipper began a slow descent for the strict purpose of honouring his promise to the passengers, that we would endeavour to find the legendary Bor herd. Most flying boat types will doubtless recall tales of this large herd of elephants, said to roam the area bordering the marshes. In those early post-war days the number of aircraft flying through was far too low for there to be any other than a primitive form of air traffic control, indeed this was purely advisory for flight watch purposes. Certainly there was never any thought or serious consideration of aircraft separation as so few aeroplanes were airborne at a given time in any one sector. This situation was what enabled us to act as free agents and to go elephant hunting if we so wished.

In fact, we descended down to around 1,000 feet and sometimes lower, whilst hurtling over the high green marsh growth which I took to be elephant grass whilst the passengers stood alongside the windows of the observation lounge peering hard for their first glimpse of the herd. On this, and subsequent occasions, large groups of these great beasts were clearly visible, and I still retain poor quality photographs in which they can, nonetheless, be seen. These were delightful episodes in flight, and of course along with others, were what made this aeroplane and route so popular with our passengers.

Object achieved, it was then back to cruising height again and on to Juba, with our way off to the east, and marked by masses of thunder cloud, the high ground leading on and up to the Abyssinian (now Ethiopian) highlands.

With southerly progress, the greenery increased, as did the volume of water and, at times, map-reading became slightly more difficult with the increase in tributaries and odd whorls in the river's path not, as far as could be determined, marked on the early maps which we used.

The ground below moved progressively closer to us, for we were approaching the plateau area and our destination, Port Bell, was in the region of 5,000 feet above sea level. Port Bell was a small area of water on the north shore of Lake Victoria, just to the east of Kampala and was little more than a mooring site, virtually on the Equator. I do not recall how or why this spot was chosen as our transit base or night stop but it was one of the prettiest and most enjoyable spots that we could ever wish to use on that trip down to Johannesburg.

Our accommodation was in African-style whitewashed circular huts with a kind of thatched roof and the site itself was known as Silver Springs, a title which it retained for many years and for all I know may still do so.

Sleeping, relaxing and dining were all under ideal conditions and so pleasant were the surroundings that if one ever thought of retirement or a retirement home this just had to be the spot.

When I look at what has happened in Central Africa today, I am bewildered. In 1947, whatever their colour, race or creed, everyone in that part of the world always seemed happy with their lot and smiles abounded. I was saddened many years later, when passing through the same area, to be greeted by sullen looks and curt responses to any attempt at friendly conversation. So much for independence and politicians certainly have a lot to answer for I suspect.

Anyway it is all history now, but nonetheless I have many happy memories of this part of the world. Life flowed at a sensible pace and was spent in parkland surroundings cooled by balmy breezes off the Lake and all of this right on the Equator. Gloom and doom merchants will remind me of the rainy season and things could indeed be vastly different at such times of the year but these I prefer to forget, as they weren't of any great consequence.

After a delightful overnight rest, we were up at the crack of dawn and off southwards again.

The take-off altitude, as I have previously observed, did have some adverse effect on engine performance. However, provided the windspeed and direction were not too critical, once off the mooring, the boat could be headed south and throttles opened ready for take-off. It mattered not if it seemed to take ages to become unstuck: one had hundreds of miles of Lake Victoria ahead in which to become airborne. In those days, BOAC had alternative marine sites available on the lake, one to the east at Kisumu and another on the southern shore at Mwanza.

Our track down to Victoria Falls, our next exotic night stop, ran across Lake Tanganyika, passing south of Ujiji, and from then on the ground below conjured up many thoughts of the great works of Doctor Livingstone in that part of the world. In fact one of our party pieces, just as with the Bor herd, was to keep a watchful eye open for Lake Bangeulo and as it hove into sight, to descend gently so that by the time we passed it by, it was all eyes down for first sight of Chitambo's Village, where I believe Livingstone died, and where his heart is buried.

The ground features south from Lake Victoria now followed a reverse pattern starting with rich green in the north, slowly becoming a brown or yellow surface of scrub as one passed across the copper belt towards the Zambezi. Still a fair measure of green here and there but not as marked as further north.

The average flight time to the Falls was seven hours but while still thirty minutes short of destination the crew would be looking ahead for the first sign of the 'smoke which thunders' – the native name for the Falls.

I still remember my first sighting, since from afar I thought I was seeing smoke from a bush fire, but the skipper soon put me right. What I was seeing was the spray flung way into the air as the Zambezi plunged into the gorge.

Inevitably, before landing a few miles up the Zambezi from the Falls, a couple of low level circuits over the top were a must. To fully appreciate the beauty and power they must be seen from the air. On this occasion I did go along on a ground trip to view the Falls from the Devil's Cataract end and whilst the sheer mass of water pouring over the top and the accompanying roar left one speechless, the view from the air, when the whole panorama can be seen at one glance, is unbelievable in its beauty.

We alighted and moored a few miles up stream from the Falls, but our journey to the hotel was delayed because a rogue elephant had decided to tear up the newly-erected telephone poles and toss them over the road. Overnight accommodation was provided for passengers and crew at the famous Victoria Falls Hotel, which as far as rooms and furniture were concerned still belonged in the time of the Queen of the same name. Facilities were immediately provided to take us down to the Falls and the bridge over the gorge and a meaningful description of both could only come from a gifted writer, not from me. All I can say is that this, and subsequent visits, left a permanent, happy and colourful picture in my mind.

Since the irrepressible Bunny Austin of Augusta fame was responsible for catering at the hotel this left nothing to be desired. We spent a pleasant evening on the terrace, watching baboons who came closer

66

and closer in the twilight, until eventually the braver ones would whip scraps of food off the table if one did not remain alert.

A short hop the next day, down to Johannesburg with the first part of the three and a half hour flight over scrubland and then part desert, until reaching the mountainous region to the north of our destination.

I recall that our Captain, a jovial eccentric, hearing that this was my first trip to this part of the world, asked me to keep him up to date with the estimated time of reaching the Limpopo, the dreaded Limpopo, the crocodile river. Taken in completely, I beavered away to provide an updated estimated time and when we finally saw the river ahead he called me up and said 'I want you to see if you can spot my topee'. I could hardly believe what I was hearing when he added 'I lost the bloody thing when I crossed the Limpopo on Safari in 1940'.

The penny did finally drop as I glanced round and spotted the evil bunch behind me smothering their laughter: they'd heard it all before. That was one of the many games played by this man who finally became a minister of the Church and retired to Africa to work, would you believe.

The nearest alighting spot to Johannesburg for us was the massive Lake of Vaaldam, created by damming the Vaal River which formed the border of the Orange Free State and the Transvaal. Arrival procedures completed we were then driven up to Johannesburg, where in a modern hotel and in what was so obviously a major business centre, we spent a restful day, part of which was given over, as always, to shopping.

This was my first experience of seeing the open separation of black and white, emphasised all the more to us on the Friday morning when we were taken to one of the mine compounds, to watch the natives, Zulus I believe, dance. I think I should refrain from further description at this moment.

There was a problem at Vaaldam which I experienced for the first time and that was a so called 'glassy calm' water condition for alighting. In such circumstances, it was extremely difficult to judge height and quite often our launches had to cross and recross the alighting area to create at least some surface disturbance and thereby assist the captain by providing a better visual check on height in the closing stages of landing. One amusing anecdote concerns a captain who shall remain anonymous. In calm conditions he had watched his co-pilot make several abortive attempts to land and taking over he said 'I'll show you how to land in glassy calm conditions'.

Making a steady approach he assumed that he had finally put the flying boat down and being satisfied with the outcome of his efforts, he released the control column saying to his first officer 'There you are, that's how it should be done'. An instant later, the great boat which was in fact still a few feet up in the air dropped with an earth shattering crash on to the water, sending spray everywhere. The sequel does not matter but the moral does and that chap became a little older and hopefully a little wiser on that day.

Oddly enough, it was at Vaaldam that I witnessed the effects of damage to a wing float. We had a rather heavy landing and having disembarked our passengers, we were about to step out on to the launch when we noticed that we were stepping up rather than out. A quick glance to the other side of the aeroplane set alarm bells ringing when we saw that the starboard float was almost under water. It had fractured on landing and was rapidly filling up with water.

Following the Captain and under his shouted orders, we raced back to the flight deck, out through the roof hatch, to crawl carefully out towards the port wing tip. Our combined weights caused the other wing to tilt up and keep the opposite float from submerging, until hastily summoned launch crews took the necessary remedial action. Life was certainly different for aviators in those days.

I spent two whole years, I think probably the happiest in my aviation career, travelling to and fro in these gentle giants, skippered by gentlemen aviators.

Many of our captains were a law unto themselves and as an example I recall on one occasion the flying boat which we were crewing being taken out from the loading dock in Alexandria to allow a certain incoming captain to bring his own boat in to refuel and be on his way. He was just in a hurry, and he had the right surname. Another transported a jeep back in pieces one trip after another from Africa to the UK and this was done over a period of two months.

A third, the archetypal colonial officer, wherever he went, and this included first-class hotels in Europe, insisted on calling all male staff 'bearer', the Indian title for a servant. On my first visit to Japan, where due to General MacArthur's refusal to allow BOAC further on, we had to land at Iwakuni, close by Hiroshima, this captain used all his power to assist me with a shopping problem. Incidentally the aftermath of Hiroshima has been well chronicled so I won't refer to what we saw.

Japanese bone china tea services were the 'in thing' in 1949, but our arrival was after shop closing hours. Hearing of my dilemma, in that I had no way of making a purchase since we were off early in the morning, he said 'Come with me lad, I'll sort this out'.

Still in BOAC uniform, he approached an unsuspecting Australian NCO, one of the occupying military staff at Iwakuni, and speaking as if he were an Admiral of the Fleet, and he probably looked it, he said 'Look here my man' and he then spelled out the problem to the Aussie.

I know that the Aussies are no great respecters of authority and our man was in reality only a civilian but such was his overpowering presence and voice, that within an hour I had my bone china tea service.

What happy days and what characters we flew with. All long gone now I am afraid. As I write, I find the incidents and anecdotes come rushing back but as they would fill a book they are best not repeated, since they would risk creating boredom. One thing is for sure that for me they formed a major part of my life and I can still chuckle to myself as I think them over. In August 1949 I made what was to be my last trip in a flying boat.

The then Chairman of BOAC, Whitney Strait, had come to the not unreasonable conclusion that aeroplanes had to fly to make money, and fat, comfortable low passenger capacity flying boats, sitting on the water overnight could not do that.

So inevitably the flying boat fleet was to be wound up, the boats sold and the crews moved over to flying machines with wheels which needed concrete on which to land.

Most of the boats were sold to the Aquila Airways Company and a number of the captains decided to go with them but I and my navigator colleagues were informed that we were to join the Argonaut Fleet based at London, the Argonaut being an updated four-engined Douglas aircraft, now powered by Rolls-Royce Merlin engines.

CHAPTER 5

WHEELS AND CONCRETE

S o it was that shortly after Christmas 1949, I reported to Meadowbank, an old country house on the Bath Road close by Heathrow, which had been set up to accommodate a ground training unit, to deal with the rapid influx of newly appointed Argonaut crews.

Little did I know that not too many months hence, I would become a member of that training team myself, but at present, I and my colleagues had to go through the indoctrination process dealing with the operation of a modern type of aircraft, the Argonaut, with updated on board navigational aids, and of course one which was far faster than the dear old flying boat.

For we web-footed creatures there was also the matter of adjusting to the problems associated with operating out of limited airfield space where aircraft performance now became a far more important factor. However, that was more a matter for the men up front.

Incidentally, referring to these men up front and before finally leaving the subject of flying boats, there is an amusing little anecdote concerning the 'reverse' conversion of one captain from land planes to flying boats, in the mid-40s.

Having spent his career thus far flying conventional machines, one particular captain, whilst carrying out a conversion course on to flying boats from the base at Hythe, unexpectedly commenced a final approach for a landing at the airfield at Hurn, close by Bournemouth.

Brought to a halt by the shocked flying boat training captain, the trainee apologised for his dreadful oversight, blaming it entirely on his many years of carrying out approaches to airfields in landplanes and somewhat shamefacedly assured his instructor that this would never happen again. He then flew the flying boat back to Southampton Water, made a perfect 'landing' on the sea and jumping out of his seat, opened the hatch and with a smile and a quick glance back stepped straight over the side into the water.

Flight planning now formed a more important part of the navigator's training syllabus and since the routes on which we were to operate included long trans-desert flights, there was an even greater emphasis on the use of astronomical aids. Finally of course, gone were the pleasant lengthy stopovers, shared with passengers, for we were now back to the slip crew system involving a maximum reasonable day's flying and then, after landing at an en route airfield, a hand-over to another crew, whilst we then waited for the next aircraft through and a like hand-over.

This system still allowed some time to enjoy the pleasures of the various places involved, but no time to get to know our passengers. It also meant of course that one could leave London, crewing an aircraft bound for say Nairobi but, after hand-over, find that the next aircraft in your hands was destined for Karachi.

It was all very involved, but after a while, most of us became past masters at interpreting the complicated 'slip' graphs which traced our movements from one aircraft to another, although if an aeroplane became delayed for any reason, the whole pattern broke down.

Early in January I was rostered to join a crew due to operate out to Lydda (Israel) and back, via Rome both ways, all in a period of three days, and unfortunately only transitting the eternal city, as a refuelling spot.

It was interesting to have a lengthy overnight stay in Tel Aviv, because the last time I had visited was in 1945 when, with the RAF, I had been involved in flying King Abdullah home to his new Kingdom of Jordan.

These were obviously hard times for the Israelis, the Hotel accommodation, said to be the best, was still very primitive and the food decidedly basic.

I was a little upset that, en route, all I saw of Rome was from the air although as time progressed it was included in our schedules as a night stop station and what happy times we then had there, but more of that later.

After Tel Aviv, I found myself heading further east, although on this occasion only as far as Kuwait. The route of course no longer held any great interest for me, having now flown it whilst in the RAF and subsequently in flying boats, but some of the stopover points were new.

On the outbound flight, with a refuelling stop at Rome, we handed over our aeroplane at Damascus and since passenger services through that particular point were infrequent, we found ourselves with a stopover of almost four complete days. I shall never forget that stay, not only for the many historical attractions in the ancient city, but also because of the friendliness of everyone we met from officials down to street traders. A far cry from the situation today.

On my first day, I set off with a few crew members who were already familiar with the city, and on their assurance that it was quite safe to do so, I pressed on into the old city by myself. I first walked the ancient 'Street called Straight' and marvelled at the variety and age of the dwellings and crafts.

The bordering streets and alleys teemed with people and although one was jostled endlessly, there was no evidence of bad temper or vindictiveness as everyone seemed intent on going about their business. Quite a few of the streetside alcoves were full of Arabs, sipping cups of coffee and pulling endlessly on their 'hubble bubble' pipes, whilst shouting and gesticulating to add to the general hubbub.

I noticed quite a few of them wrapped in cream coloured robes with hoods or forms of turbans on top of their heads, their tanned faces, wrinkles and all, seemed to have been carved out of mahogany. They could only be the Bedouin, in from the Great Desert, for what purpose one can only guess. In the midst of this wandered the odd goat or two, searching, nibbling and being booted on as they made their way forward, added to which diminutive donkeys, ladened like juggernauts, were constantly thrashed by their owners, hell bent on urging them forward through the crowds. From all of this came a far from unpleasant aroma, a mixture beyond description.

At one stage, I espied a blazing oven inside an earthen-walled house and looking in I spotted the wrinkled smiling face of an old Arab, who beckoned to me. No way could one hesitate or refuse such a friendly gesture, so in I went. Neither one of us had the foggiest idea of what each was trying to convey in words to the other but I pointed into the beehive style oven, whereupon he passed a huge wooden paddle in and removed something from the roof of the hot chamber. It turned out to be a form of pancake, but the taste whilst still warm, was delicious.

Wherever I wandered, and I certainly moved well off the beaten track, equally friendly faces greeted me. I don't know how, but I eventually found myself in the back streets of the market area, all of which were covered in a manner very similar to English shopping arcades. Trades operated in separate areas and I was fascinated by the rich brocades, beautifully made carpets, endless stalls selling spices and finally by the perfume market.

Here, the traders were selling pure essences, and extracts and I still have a small phial of jasmine, which to this day, over forty years later, when the stopper is carefully prised off, retains its rich aroma.

There is no way I could remember how I eventually came out of the old town to the west, but when I did I honestly felt that I had just been transported back over the centuries and, walking on to the bottom end of town what a dreadful anticlimax that was. Describing this visit to a business man who had visited Syria recently, his only remark was that in this day and age I would probably have my throat cut a few steps after entering the old city and my clothes would be on sale at a street stall soon after. Such is progress.

Around this time, BOAC had commenced flights through Beirut also, using it as a slip crew point, but since the frequency of services was very low it proved uneconomical to leave crews sitting on the ground twiddling their thumbs for up to one week in Beirut. As a consequence therefore, crews handing over aircraft at Beirut or Damascus, were transported from one airfield to another in order to maintain the frequency of services from both and hence also gain maximum utilisation of staff. This proved to be most advantageous to us for, as an example, after landing at say Damascus, we would have a night's rest, followed by a colourful and interesting ride through the fertile valley area to the east of Beirut, over the mountains and then down to the coast, where at the famed Bristol Hotel we could spend a delightful few days resting, seabathing or sightseeing in the city before taking the next aircraft on and eastwards out of Beirut.

On more than one occasion, we were taken back into the valley to the east of Beirut to visit Baalbek and the surrounding country where ancient temples and ruins brought history to life.

Since the incoming crew from the west also preferred the comfort of Beirut to the more austere accommodation in Damascus, they were allowed to rest in Beirut and were only transported eastwards over the mountains to Damascus, shortly before their scheduled takeover time at that point.

Many of my subsequent flights simply took me over old ground again, until eventually, BOAC commenced flights to Singapore via Colombo.

My first such trip was routed via Bombay, which I had previously seen only from the air as we approached, or took off after refuelling. On this occasion since the newly opened route was covered solely on a weekly basis, we spent a full seven days sampling all that Bombay had to offer, not that this amounted to much, but fortunately it was well out of the south-west monsoon season.

I suppose, bearing in mind that overseas holiday travel for British citizens had not yet taken off, we were extremely lucky to have access to the full facilities of the beach club, where a cool swimming pool, plenty of good food and drink, endless sun, turned our stopover into a mini holiday.

From Bombay our outward flight took us southwards, hugging, but crossing and recrossing, the west coast of India, flying over travel brochure-style palm-fringed beaches until, in the region of the Portuguese settlement of Goa, we turned half left, across the southern tip of India and on to what was then Ceylon. There, we were again fortunate enough to be accommodated in one of the best hotels, in this case the Mount Lavinia, situated virtually on the seashore, on a rocky promontory, south of the city of Colombo.

Like so many of the older hotels in the East it had an air of Victorian times about it. Heavy teak furniture and fittings, the mandatory 'king-sized' juddering ceiling fans, endless staff to attend to one's every need and good wholesome colonial style food. It was but a few steps from our rooms down on to the smooth sandy beach, bordered by coconut palms and washed by thundering surf.

So, once settled on to a raffia mat on the white sand, it was holiday time again and when thirsty, one of the attendant bearers would scale a palm, acquire a coconut, hack off the top and the sweet milk was there on tap as a light refreshment. Surf boards were supplied although I do recall, as so often happened with a high surf, that there was a severe undertow against which one had to be on guard at all times.

Colombo proved to be a pleasant enough city as the citizens were friendly, but it lacked any attractive shopping sites or worthwhile goods to buy and so after one visit, the tendency was to remain in or about the hotel until departure time.

I must confess that I was intrigued to see elephants working here and there in adjacent plantations, giant placid beasts who seemed to work endlessly without any visible form of complaint when goaded on by their 'drivers'.

The whole area was very green and bore a great similarity to many parts of India, not surprisingly I suppose. All in all, a very pleasant and restful stopover point but onwards we had to go and in due time we were off at sunrise for the next stage and our final overseas destination, Singapore.

Shortly after sunrise, the weather was clear, but off to the east could be seen large cumulo-nimbus clouds, marking the Inter-Tropical Front, to which I have referred earlier on in this narrative.

Of course, the Argonaut, having a higher ceiling and better overall performance than the flying boat, enabled us to gain a much higher altitude very quickly, although even then, such was the vertical cloud development in the tropics, there was often no way in which one could top the weather. This meant ploughing through the thunderstorms whilst being tossed all over the sky. Far more unpleasant than riding down below in a flying boat. Ridiculous though it may sound as one plunged into the murk and it became darker and darker, as often happened at night also, the cockpit lights were turned fully on, so that the all-essential flight instruments could be monitored and then, fingers crossed, anal muscles clenched tight, through we would go. Looked at seriously, what were the options? To turn back just wasn't on, not for reasons of bravado, but simply because there were other approaches which could be adopted. Going higher didn't work because in that part of the world the thunder cloud tops went way beyond our ceiling. A descent could have led to far more turbulence and no guarantee that the cloud base would permit flight below, plus the fact that there was more chance of getting hammered by hail down there and, in any event, fuel consumption would have been adversely affected.

The more one came to appreciate the strength and staying power of the Argonaut, the more one could adjust to flying in such conditions and eventually most of us became blasé or resigned. There wasn't much else we could have done anyway.

Our initial track was practically due east across the Indian Ocean, heading for Sabang, an old ship's coaling station on an island which sits at the northern tip of Sumatra.

Of course there was nothing to be seen from the air for hours and hours, apart from blue tropical ocean, when cloud permitted, and occasional ships which were following the same route as us, between Colombo and Malaysia or Indonesia.

The only navigational aids were two radio beacons, one situated in the Nicobar Islands off to the north, and the other behind us at Colombo, but our sextant could be used for taking sun and, where possible, moon sights, yes the moon by day, and thus obtain useful position lines.

Weather permitting, there was never any trouble in sighting the coast of Sumatra and eventually in picking up signals from a very low-powered radio beacon sited at Sabang.

Once overhead Sabang, we would take up a south-easterly heading, flying down the Straits of Malacca with the coast of Sumatra to our right and way off to the east, the faint outline of the Malaysian Peninsular, highlighted by masses of cloud sitting on top.

As we progressed south the two great land masses converged until finally, we were hugging the Malaysian coastline on down and into Singapore. At that time the authorities were in the process of completing a new airport and the old service aerodromes had been returned to their rightful owners.

Once on the ground, the routine was pretty much as it had been in flying boat days, with the same hotel, the same recreational centre and above all the same drinking and shopping spots.

Since the Argonaut fleet had taken over from the flying boat team, the routes out of Singapore were precisely as before. Either home again by the reverse route or up to Bangkok and on to Hong Kong, before finally turning westward. When flying on to Hong Kong we found that the airfield and staff at Bangkok, our en route refuelling point, were modern and effective, but at Hong Kong it was a different story.

Accustomed to a leisurely approach to the colony, with the occasional possibility of landing well outside and then taxying into the port, we now had the major problem of landing on the original short runway at Kai Tak with no alternative site other than a diversion to the far away Philippines at Manila.

The only approach to the short runway at Kai Tak was over the built up area of Kowloon, passing close by high rise bedroom windows on the descent and then a controlled dive at the runway. I won't elaborate other than to say that every landing was a new experience and if anyone who knows the set-up at Hong Kong at this present time can visualise a shorter runway directed further away from the sea, and using far less powerful aeroplanes, can probably just begin to see our problem – and do bear in mind that even now the colony is having a new aerodrome built, as the present one is considered far too limiting. In our days this present so-called limiting runway would have been a much sought after luxury. Happy days they were, and in spite of the difficulties we had jolly good times and I don't recall any serious accidents at Hong Kong, other than the odd unplanned bowel movement on some of the final approaches.

For two whole years from May 1950, my time was spent in flying to and from the Near and Far East, during which period all the odd things which can happen to an aeroplane did so to the Argonaut, although at no time was there anything more serious than an occasional engine failure and since the aeroplane could cope quite adequately on three engines, most of our crew members grew to like and respect the Argonaut, almost as much as the dear old flying boat.

During this period, there was one unique incident which I reckon very few flying types have experienced. Descending, on an approach to Karachi, with everything seemingly in order and the prospect of a cool glass of beer not too far ahead, there was suddenly a loud bang at the front of the aircraft and a huge yellow patch appeared on one of the front windscreens, partially obscuring vision. Initial reaction was that we had hit a bird, but before we could give further thought to the matter, there was a series of even louder bangs and, as if by magic, the whole front screen was totally obliterated by a thick yellow mass, almost as if some unseen body had tipped gallons of yellow emulsion paint over the front of the aeroplane.

Fortunately for us, it was still possible to see out of both side flight deck windows, and being unpressurised by now, we were able to open these windows and for the pilots to thus gain limited vision. We made an emergency radio call to the ground controller at Karachi, since by now we were on the final approach to landing, when the jolly little fellow down below, who seemed to think it amusing, said that all aircraft were to be warned of a locust swarm to the west of the airfield.

Well, at least that answered the question of what it was all about, but it required a great deal of skill for the Captain, who would have liked to pop his head out of the side window, but couldn't, to put this machine back down on to terra firma, without damage. To his credit, and with no direct forward vision, he did just that without the passengers realising that anything untoward had occurred. Another one-off memorable incident.

I was involved in a run of services to Baghdad and back, which fortunately for me allowed a few days in Damascus either on the outbound or homeward flight, and as a consequence I was able to spend more and more time in the old city which fascinated me beyond belief. I have read Doughty's *Arabia Deserta* recently and he captures and describes the beauty of that city and its cosmopolitan citizens far better than I ever could, but I can understand exactly what he is trying to convey having experienced it myself.

By late 1950 BOAC had pushed further north from Hong Kong and we now regularly operated to Tokyo, with Okinawa as a refuelling point on the way. Fortunately we were able to use one of the United States Air Force Military bases at Naha, on Okinawa, where their facilities matched those of major airports anywhere in the world. Where else, so soon after the war, could you walk into a PX shop and buy virtually anything, and then move on to their canteen, for want of a better word, for a three course meal, rounded off with apple pie *à la mode* with fresh cream or ice cream.

Elsewhere, a ham sandwich was the most that a transit crew could expect. On top of this, their Armed Forces Radio Network pumped out wonderful programmes to suit all and sundry 24 hours a day. Oh! those Yanks, they sure know how to organise things.

In Tokyo, they had arranged first-class hotels for civil and military crews and had made life in that city a true home from home.

I recall that wherever we stayed the Americans had stand-by arrangements for female company, if one was so inclined, but it was all far more discreet than their call girl system back home in the States. I can honestly say, with hand on heart, that I never attempted to avail myself of this facility. However, I do recall the price which one co-pilot paid for his interest.

He was told that if he placed his shoes outside his room door and draped a towel over the door handle, this was the recognised signal that company was needed. He did just that, but to the amusement of the rest of the crew, the only response he obtained was to have his shoes and towel stolen.

On one refuelling stop at Okinawa we experienced a rather unique event. Starting up for departure we found that the starter motor for one of the starboard engines was dead and as a consequence we had to shut down the others and seek help. Being Rolls-Royce engines, the American Air Force had no spare parts and hence we had to signal Hong Kong for a spare starter motor from our maintenance unit there, to be flown up. They certainly had the spare part, but as no aircraft was coming our way from Hong Kong for the next 48 hours, we were stuck.

This presented a problem, for much as our American friends would have loved to share the company of our lady passengers, they had no suitable accommodation for them on a military base, although doubtless the more amorous and resourceful ones could have solved that problem.

Anyway, their engineering people came up with two bright suggestions. The first was to obtain a length of stout rope to which was attached a leather cap. This was placed over a propeller tip on the sick engine and then several hefty men gave the rope a mighty tug, whilst the ignition switch was fired at the appropriate time. Needless to say this ingenious idea did not work, so on to the second.

With our passengers standing by on the tarmac, we started up three engines and moved out on to the huge runway. At a given signal we roared down the runway, heading for a possible three-engined take-off, with the hope that the propeller on the fourth engine would start to windmill so that we could then induce that engine to fire.

If by any chance it did so, then depending on where this happened, we could either abandon take-off, or take off and return after a quick circuit of the airfield, and either way, we hoped to return with all four engines running, so that our passengers could then be hastened on board, and away we could go. This attempt also proved abortive and in fact the propeller never budged, even when we reached up to 80 knots forward speed.

It is quite incredible, in this day and age, to even contemplate such ideas, but the war was not so far back, and it was part of the left over spirit, which caused us to make this somewhat drastic and crazy attempt.

Fortunately a short while later, another signal arrived to say that a spare starter motor had been placed on an American Military Air Transport DC-7 which was coming our way and it was with us before nightfall. There was a struggle to get it fitted, as the Americans were not familiar with the Merlin engine and we did not carry a flight engineer on the Argonaut. However, with superb co-operation all round, it was successfully fitted and we were away after dark for the final stage up to Tokyo.

We only missed Okinawa, on the way to Tokyo, on one occasion and that was when Sod's Law struck again. This was an occasion when one of the seasonal typhoons was fast approaching the island. Typhoons were all given lady's names and my log book recalls that this one had been christened Dinah.

As surface winds were beginning to pick up, we diverted to the north, planning to land at Iwakuni in order to refuel. Shortly before arrival at Iwakuni one of the engines started to make unhealthy noises and had to be shut down. No point in going into Iwakuni now, as they had no facilities to deal with a sick Merlin engine, and so we decided to press on knowing that we had civil aerodromes at Ōsaka and Nagoya should we need a bolt-hole, but hoping to reach Tokyo on three engines anyway. In the event, our guardian angel was with us and even at reduced speed we finally made it, much to the relief of all on board.

Again, a little of the press on spirit which prevailed at that time, but which today is just not on, indeed the law is far more stringent now and precludes any such action.

Life remained very pleasant for the period between mid-1950 and 1952, and then improved somewhat when BOAC commenced operations further south and south-west from the United Kingdom, in fact to South America.

However, before leaving the Eastern routes there remained one more somewhat worrying flight. In the mid-fifties, Iran was controlled by the zealous Mossadeq, and fired with national pride and other reasons which historians will relate, he threatened to nationalise the Iranian oilfields and boot out all operating staff who were not nationals.

In spite of much diplomatic activity the balloon burst and he carried out his threat, accompanied by many less savoury ones.

The British Navy went in and sailing up from the Gulf into the mouth of the Shatt al Arab, anchored threateningly alongside and then successfully evacuated staff of the Anglo Iranian Oil Company, from the giant refinery at Ābādān.

Unfortunately, but with great courage, a team of doctors and nurses remained behind, presumably to deal with last minute medical problems and cases.

So it was that on 3 October 1951, I was one of an Argonaut crew who were told, in a quiet matter of fact way, that we were to fly into Ābādān and bring out these last remaining staff.

The international atmosphere was extremely tense with much sabre rattling from Mossadeq and we were most apprehensive to say the least. There would be no problem locating the airfield, but as to our reception, no one had a clue what lay ahead. All we were told was that a cruiser, HMS *London* I think it was, was anchored in the river nearby, but how that was expected to help us I never did discover.

In the event, we made an exploratory run over what seemed to be a deserted airfield and as no one shot at us, we decided to go on in.

The place was indeed deserted and as we came to a halt, leaving the engines ticking over: a lonely Iranian trundled a set of aircraft steps out and the medical people piled on board. I do recall that we had to prevent one chap from bringing a hand-pushed lawn mower on board. Goodness knows what it was doing in that desert region and it is probably still there. Odd people the Brits!

We wasted no time in getting airborne again and by way of celebration, having first flown by to identify ourselves, we followed up with a fast low level beat-up of the nearby cruiser, and then off across the desert to home.

CHAPTER 6

COPACOBANA AND
ALL THAT SORT OF THING

Prior to the commencement of BOAC services to South America, this route had been operated by British South American Airways using converted wartime Lancaster aircraft which were then known as Lancastrians, and later by the ill fated Avro Tudor, which also flew to the Central Caribbean.

The late great Don Bennett was then in charge of affairs and there is little doubt that he established a smooth efficient service to South America, well supported by loyal crews, but with aeroplanes which in truth were hardly suitable for the job.

The many misfortunes of this company and the aircraft losses are well recorded so I will not dwell on them in this narrative.

As is known, BOAC and BSAA merged in the early 50s at which point the Argonauts took over the South American route.

For my part, I was delighted, when in July 1952 I found myself rostered to operate out to Santiago, Chile, via the South Atlantic route, and here started another most enjoyable phase in my flying career, for every stage was new, all the stopover points were most pleasant, and thanks to BSAA staff, en route facilities of every kind, were of the best.

On 13 July 1952 we departed from Heathrow for the somewhat lengthy first day. A four hour flight down to Madrid, where station staff handed us a bottle of sherry each as a gift from the export agent, then a short hop across to Lisbon, followed by another four hour haul down to Dakar in Sénégal. This sector, I had last flown in the RAF, but it remained as before, a fair weather run, paralleling the coast of Morocco and Spanish and French West Africa, with easily recognisable coastal landmarks and good reliable radio beacons on the way, until our arrival on time at the delightful stopover point of Dakar, where the waiting crew took over to operate the next two sectors to Recife in Northern Brazil and then on down to Rio de Janeiro.

Since the city of Dakar was comparatively undeveloped by present day standards, our hotel accommodation was very basic but it was comfortable and the food was good. By way of compensation, transport was readily available to take us the few short miles to Ngor Beach, a stretch of fine sand, with warm sea and surf, where we spent most of our time between flights relaxing and mopping up the sunshine.

At Dakar, I discovered a well-established flight crew trading system in operation, whereby almost any quality liqueur could be purchased at bargain prices and then transported to Rio, where a somewhat seedy caretaker, who looked after our accommodation there, would trade the drink for top quality perfumes, the major one being Aupège, I think.

Whilst relaxing at Dakar, I had time to contemplate the forth-coming flight to Recife, which would be totally over the South Atlantic and involve two major factors: the first was simply that there were no radio aids whatsoever on the crossing other than a non-directional beacon at Dakar and a much lower powered version of the same, at Recife; the second involved the dreaded Inter-Tropical Front.

As I have already described, this convergence zone produced atrocious weather which apart from the masses of cloud, rain and hail, threw up some of the severest thunderstorms any of us had ever experienced. Unfortunately for us, this line of bad weather lay at a very shallow angle to our track, hence it often became necessary to make a sharp alteration of heading in order to cross the zone at right angles and minimise the time spent being thrown all over the sky.

The only navigational aid for the long crossing, was the sextant, and provided weather conditions permitted, astronomical fixes could be planned at hourly intervals.

When one reflects upon this crossing and of the associated navigational and weather problems, it is impossible not to have the greatest admiration for that New Zealand lady pioneer, Jean Batten, who made this crossing in a single-engined aircraft, long before our big four-engined ships came along.

Duly rested, we were informed a couple of days later, that our aero-plane had departed from Lisbon on time, so we bathed, dressed in our BOAC livery, ate and set off for the airfield to make preparations.

The calculated flight time to Recife was eight and a half hours and the weather man took great delight in telling us that we should meet the bad weather at the half way point. I suppose he could afford to smile; after all he was returning to a snug warm bed after we had departed.

Around midnight, we commenced our long, rumbling take-off run, in the tropical heat, and sat fingers crossed as the runway lights flashed by at an increasing rate until, with the red distance warning lights ahead, the faithful Argonaut eased gently into the air. Straight out over the sea, with nothing but water ahead now, we commenced the long slow climb to our cruising altitude.

There wasn't much that I, as a navigator, could do other than to note the angle between our stern and the radio compass needle pointing towards the Dakar radio beacon, since this would give a pretty good indication of the angle at which we were drifting off our compass heading. This would show the track which we were actually making good, a most useful piece of information for the first hour out.

Once at cruising height, I would set about my astronomical observations, using a far more sophisticated sextant than those I had been accustomed to in RAF days.

The system used was based upon the work of a gentleman named Marc St Hilaire, whereby using an assumed ground position, at a pre-determined time, and extracting values from a volume of star data, the navigator calculated the bearings of three stars and also their altitudes. Sextant sights were then made and the actual altitude values noted and compared with the pre-calculated values.

If an observed altitude was greater than the calculated, it indicated that the observer was closer to the stars' zenith than assumed and a short calculation then enabled the navigator to plot a line of position. Three such lines, with bearings roughly 120 degrees apart, would hopefully all pass through the same point on the chart and thus determine the aircraft position. In practice, since minor errors in sighting often occurred, the resultant position lines formed a triangle, appropriately called by navigators a 'cocked hat', and the position was assumed to be in the centre of this triangle.

Anyway, off into the black night we went and after about an hour's flying, the stars began to disappear behind thin high cloud, while on the far horizon, ominous yellow flashes could be seen, heralding our approach to the Inter-Tropical Front.

The pattern was invariably the same. A gradual thickening of cloud, a little light rain from above at first, slowly increasing in intensity as we approached the front and then into the thick dense cumulus cloud with lightning increasing ahead.

As the weather deteriorated and heavy turbulence indicated that cumulo-nimbus storm clouds were present, up went the cockpit lights to exclude some of the visible signs of mother nature's bad temper and then having reduced air speed to a safe cloud and turbulence penetration value, we would effectively batten down the hatches, turn directly into the storm and aim for a quick right angled penetration.

Passengers were normally advised to expect a short spell of unpleasant turbulence, although unpleasant was the understatement of all time, and I know from the odd occasion when I went aft to see how things were, that most, other than a few veterans, were absolutely petrified with fear – and why not?

Quite often, after a short and severe battering, the turbulence and lightning would lessen until, to everyones relief, stars could be glimpsed above, and slowly but surely we would fly out into clear air and resume the required heading, with all the activity now off to the starboard or right side of the aeroplane.

Occasionally a homebound aircraft would be operating the same sector at the same time and we would endeavour to contact them using the radio telephony system, in order to exchange information on the weather, particularly areas to be avoided where possible. I suppose it gave some comfort to hear a friendly voice in the darkness when way out in mid-Atlantic and hundreds of miles from safety.

We normally experienced morning twilight, or first light as we called it, about two-thirds of the way across and this invariably coincided with an almost ritualistic procedure. Way out, hundreds of miles from Recife, a small pinnacle of rock jutted out into the South Atlantic, St Paul's Rocks. Whether these could be seen or not depended very much on the state of the sea, which if particularly rough, threw up clearly visible breakers.

The custom, particularly with ex-BSAA captains was to challenge the navigator to determine an accurate estimate of the time of arrival over the rocks and then if they were not visible at that time to carry on happily with stories of how they always spotted the rocks in the old days when pilots navigated on these routes.

So, shortly before the estimated time, it would be all eyes ahead, straining to seek out this tiny point of land jutting out from the otherwise dark empty and uninviting sea. I recall that I did succeed on more than one occasion and it was always a proud moment when one did so, but still an anticlimax because the pinnacle was minute and it came and went almost in an instant.

That behind us, it was usually a quiet run on into Recife, with dawn fast approaching and weak signals from the destination radio beacon just about audible on the aircraft radio.

Recife was very similar to many of the small coastal towns which I had seen in the Far East, but since I only had one brief night stop there during the two years of operations to South America I can recall nothing of real interest.

Refuelling was quickly carried out, as the idea was to get up and away before surface temperatures became uncomfortable. The journey south to Rio was usually uneventful, being mainly just inside, or off, the Brazilian coast, which provided excellent visual checks to mark progress.

Then on and into that great city. The vast bay, with the Sugar Loaf Mountain clearly visible, seemed reminiscent of Hong Kong, and fortunately on my first visit to Rio the whole area was bathed in sunlight and looked a veritable picture. I noticed that giant statue of Christ perched atop the hill to the rear of the city and I recall the strange, but as I found out later, true story of how it sometimes appeared in poor weather conditions.

Rio de Janeiro suffered from similar weather conditions as Hong Kong, in that at certain times fog and low cloud would descend, obliterating the airfield and necessitating a diversion possibly to São Paulo, but above this low cloud, and apparently emerging from it, would be seen the giant statue. Awe inspiring to say the least, but unfortunately providing no divine intervention to assist with our approach and landing: indeed it could be saying 'push off, it's no use attempting anything here today'.

We were accommodated in a high rise hotel overlooking the bustling harbour and the original, but small civil airfield which was only suitable for light aeroplanes and local traffic. The crew accommodation was almost at the top of this building and the rooms were allocated according to a long established BSAA system. Quite often, deals were struck with the radio officer to exchange his room with others, since by custom his room was always next to the stewardess and had a communicating door. This door was always kept securely locked of course!

It was on my first trip to Rio, that I was introduced to the shady waiter, or caretaker, who looked after our rooms. He could well have come straight out of an American western film, since he looked swarthy and villainous with a thick Mexican style moustache. There were invariably traces of recent meals on or around his chin and the lapels of his jacket, both of which seemed to be coated with grease. However in spite of his appearance he was pleasant enough: he had to be since he was the link man in the exchange of spirits from Dakar for the expensive perfumes, for transport home. Food in Rio was magnificent, the steaks being larger and finer than any I have seen elsewhere in the world.

I made the mandatory two-stage trip to the top of the Sugar Loaf and whilst the view was superb, the ride in the cable car both ways was far worse than any form of flying which I had known. The local citizens seemed to prance all over the car, hell bent, it would appear, on aggravating the rocking motion, which was bad enough without their assistance. Anyway, I made this pilgrimage and overall it was all worthwhile.

Likewise, one had to visit Copacobana Beach and after the drab lifestyle to which we had become accustomed back home, and elsewhere in the world, it was a revelation. One of the few places where we could see beach and beautiful Brazilian babes, totally matching all that was to be found in publicity brochures. It was not until after several visits that I managed to strike Rio at carnival time.

There is no way that I could effectively describe what happens at carnival. The Brazilians cast all inhibitions aside together with most of their clothes. They get high on anything available, and most things are, and then they give themselves entirely over to pleasure. You simply haven't lived until you have experienced *Mardi Gras* in Rio, it surpasses anything I have seen or heard before or after.

We handed our aircraft over at Rio and then relaxed until the next Argonaut came through, which we would then take on via Montevideo and Buenos Aires to our ultimate destination, Santiago, set in the western foothills of the Andes and bordering on the Chilean coast by Valparaiso.

A couple of days later, on the 19th of July to be precise, we headed south again, once more crossing territory quite new to me, but presenting nothing of real interest or difficulty. At Montevideo we were in and out in the shortest period of time as we had to refuel to the upper limit in Buenos Aires before making the crossing of the Andes.

The flight out of Buenos Aires involved a long slow climb up to our highest possible altitude, often requiring the crew to use oxygen and as maximum ceiling was approached, the rate of climb, even with full climbing power on the engines, was reduced almost to zero, so that one had virtually to give up further attempts at increasing altitude.

There were three recognised crossing points over the Andes range, the Southern, Central and Northern Passes.

These did not mean much to us, as we were way above but, from one of our ex-BSAA captains, who had previously been employed by Chilean Airways, I heard some pretty hair-raising stories of how, in atrocious weather, the locals used to fly up and through the passes, even in snow storms. Hard to believe, but I was assured that this did happen. I once saw a movie film of a journey across the Andes, through the Central Pass and that looked frightening enough, even at ground level.

BOAC became the laughing stock of most airlines in that part of the world at that time because of our supposedly over-cautious procedures. Since BSAA had lost aeroplanes on this sector, never to be found, our procedures required that ground stations were kept fully informed of our intentions and progress.

Thus it was that, having achieved maximum possible height, we would select our crossing point and then send a 'mountain attack' signal. It was this signal which caused so much amusement to the others who would just press on and over at high or low level as their fancy took them.

When I think about it years later, the BOAC move was quite in keeping with the sort of drill required of mountain climbers, and had anything gone wrong, at least search aircraft would have had some idea of where to start.

I must confess that flying above the Central Pass, with Aconcagua at some 24,000 feet in height, just off our starboard wing tip, or so it seemed, and with the aeroplane wallowing almost on the point of stall at its limiting height, it was always a relief to leave the Andes behind. Mind you, it was only a short period of crossing and then it was nose down and a very rapid descent to the foothills and the end of our journey.

At Santiago, our stopover point, we were housed in a delightful large country residence, set in an orange grove and run by a middle-aged British couple who provided all home comforts for weary crews, for it had been a long haul from Rio.

A further part of our company ruling affecting the Andes crossing was that one should not enter cloud under any circumstances. A very wise order, as I can think of nothing worse than entering cloud half way over the mountains, icing up as a consequence and then sinking down into the midst of those dark and uninviting peaks.

Strange though it may seem, on my first trip to Santiago we had clawed our way up to maximum height and had opted for the Central Pass crossing, but as we approached the Andes we began to sink into layered cloud and no way could we climb out. There was nothing for it but to turn round very quickly and head back. There was no point in flying all the way back to Buenos Aires, so on the advice of our company man in Santiago, we headed for Mendoza, a medium sized town in the eastern foothills of the Andes which had a sizeable airfield. We made an uneventful landing at this strange airfield and were made very welcome by the local staff who were not accustomed to greeting international flights. I cannot recall much of that visit, except that, of all the remarkable coincidences, the weather man who came out to brief us on the following morning had served with me at RAF Hemswell during the war and very happy he was, in this to me, remote part of the world.

Cloud conditions on the following morning precluded using the Central Pass route, but in any event we would have had to circle endlessly to gain the necessary height for that crossing, so we headed south, parallel to the Andes, climbing slowly all the way, until we reached the area of the Southern Pass, where we made an uneventful crossing to the west.

Our long haul home was simply a repeat of the outbound flight, including another hairy night crossing of the South Atlantic with its associated Inter-Tropical Front.

I did note one useful aid at the tail end of that crossing and it was the vast distance at which some of the West African coastal lights could be seen. The air light and coastal light beacons at Bathurst, at what was then the Gambia, could be seen long before our estimated arrival time at Dakar, and once identified, were a reassuring sign that the sea crossing would soon be over.

Already armed with quality perfume, plus an uplift of low priced bottles of spirit from Dakar, we eventually headed north, for home, family and a well earned rest.

During the first week of August, I was again rostered for a South American flight, which followed virtually the same schedules as before but with a couple of minor differences, or difficulties. On the outbound flight, we were routed via Lisbon, but due to certain weather problems it was necessary to land at Casablanca in order to take on more fuel. Since it was merely a rapid transit stop, I saw nothing of the city or surroundings: indeed it could have been anywhere on the globe.

A little excitement occurred at Recife outbound, when at a few hundred feet over the sea on take-off, one engine suddenly gave an enormous thump, which could be felt throughout the aeroplane, and the various gauges fluctuated madly. An order was given to feather the propeller and shut down the engine immediately, but as a measure of confidence the captain, who had allowed the co-pilot to control the take-off, now asked him to stay in control and return us to the ground. We had no need to dump fuel in order to reduce our weight, since we had a comparatively light load of fuel for the shortish sector to Rio and in any event our weight was already low, due to take-off limitations governed by the high prevailing temperatures. The first officer completed a circuit and made a text book three-engined landing, after which the ground engineers got to work on the engine.

Whatever the fault, it necessitated a night stop at Recife for us and our passengers, but neither they, or us, were particularly impressed with this spot: indeed it was just another hot sticky unscheduled stopover point.

Next morning assured by the engineers that the problem had been solved, we loaded up and moved off to the runway for take off, when one of the aircraft stewards reported smoke pouring from the one-time sick engine. Full of misery we returned to the ramp, ready to eat the ground engineer, but in the event, a quick check revealed that this would not be necessary. Although unforgivable, the fault was not mechanical, since it transpired that one of the local engineers had left a form of rubber tube, used to pick up or insert plugs, on top of the engine and once the temperature rose after start-up, it started to melt and burn the rubber. Just as well we had not got ourselves airborne, although if we had maybe we should not have seen the smoke and perhaps all would have been well anyway . . . perhaps!

CHAPTER 7

BACK TO THE EAST AND THEN BACK TO SCHOOL

On my return, thanks to the vagaries of the crew roster system, I found myself returning to the East with my first visit to Dacca, which at that time formed part of East Pakistan, I think, but other than this stop at a point so far unknown to me, the trip was a routine Eastern tour.

This was followed by another, this time to Singapore, thence operating a shuttle service up to Hong Kong and on to Tokyo via Okinawa. I must say that our out-of-town hotel in Tokyo gave us a wonderful opportunity to see a little of the real Japan, with organised visits to the many places of interest and although the country was a sight to behold on a crisp clear day with snow-covered scenery, you have not seen nature at its best until you have seen Japan in the Spring at cherry-blossom time. It truly surpasses anything I have seen before and that includes my home county of Kent at apple-blossom time.

On this particular trip it was our misfortune to find ourselves flying between Colombo and Singapore on Christmas Day and as the average traveller chooses not to do likewise, we had very few passengers on board. Catering staff had done their best and the aircraft interior was suitably decorated and an appropriate meal laid on. However, Christmas is best enjoyed at home and so we pressed on with the flight in routine fashion, but compensated in true flight crew tradition, once settled in to the Seaview Hotel in Singapore that night.

I think that most of us paid the price for our celebration on Boxing Day, when the combination of hangover and tiredness made the flight from Singapore to Hong Kong seem to take an age, although as always, somewhere south-east of Saigon, we managed to pick up the BBC World Service broadcast which cheered us up a little.

The only compensation was that we spent New Year's Day on the ground, although of all places, it had to be at Bahrain, on the way home. Never mind, the bar was well-stocked, at least it was when we started drinking, but that's another story.

Thereafter, flights became a mix of Far East and South America, but all very pleasant regardless of the routine, until in March another big change came my way.

In the early 50s, BOAC had commenced a major flight crew recruitment programme, involving a number of qualified ex-service pilots, but also many young graduates who underwent a sponsored course of training at Hamble and other professional pilot training schools situated at Oxford and Perth in Scotland. On arrival, regardless of their overall experience, these young men were immediately required to undergo a course of training with the object of obtaining a flight navigator's licence, following which they would then be required to operate as full-time navigators on all of the existing routes. BOAC certainly still carried flight navigators at that time, but this specialised training for pilots achieved a double objective. Firstly, by operating as navigators they obtained route knowledge in detail and saw their peers at work and secondly, since BOAC had already indicated that it would phase out the full-time navigating officers, these young pilots were fully prepared to take over as and when circumstances required. So it was then, that I was taken off full-time route flying and partially ground based, in order to teach these young men the theory and practice of my craft.

After a somewhat lengthy period of lectures, covering all the subjects which they required in order to obtain a flight navigator's licence, the theory was put into practice on the twin-engined de Havilland Dove aircraft. These were based at Heathrow and, assisted by a small number of staff pilots, we made daily training flights to and from Shannon in the west of Ireland. This route provided ideal basic training since it took us away from crowded United Kingdom airspace, but more importantly to us, enabled crews to purchase cheap spirits and prime steaks in Shannon on a regular basis.

When I think back to those days, I marvel at what ensued. We had to deal with some awkward, bloody-minded young men, who really only wanted to pilot aeroplanes, not to navigate them around the skies, and they made their feelings known very forcefully, yet today I see them as mature senior managers, responsible for the rapid development of one of our national airlines. In one case, a particularly outspoken trainee is now an eminent politician, not always loved by all and still giving cause for aggravation with his forthright manner, but I might add also still with a twinkle in his eye.

As training progressed and the need for more practical experience arose, navigators, like myself, who had been required to take the trainees through basic procedures, now boarded the Argonaut once more, to fly precisely the same routes as before, but this time with these young men under our wings.

We were pretty harsh on them sometimes but whatever tricks we pulled to throw them off balance, there was always a lesson to be learned and in any event, word soon got around so that in due time they were all pretty well alerted to what was likely to happen. Not that this mattered because what we did still drove home the necessary drills which we were striving to teach.

I suspect that, in due time, BOAC found this type of training rather too costly in terms of time and cash and so a genius, somewhere in the hierarchy, hit upon an alternative idea.

Why not take the dear old Avro York transport aircraft, virtually discarded by the RAF and BOAC as being past its prime, and use this aeroplane as a flying classroom. In fact, quite a few Yorks were still flying, but solely for the purpose of transporting freight and occasionally live animals.

So the project took off and the rear half of one of these flying boxes was fitted with six or eight tables, plus instruments and, in the roof, housings for the latest type of periscopic sextant. The mid- and forward-fuselage would be used for whatever needed to be transported from one place to another; crews were selected for the sole purpose of flying this noisy beast; and the whole was staffed and supervised by we navigation instructors from the training unit, with around eight or nine students on each flight.

We never knew when or where we were going until the last moment, when perhaps a call would come to transport say an engine out to a grounded aircraft somewhere in the world or maybe to pick up a load of caged birds, monkeys or even large animals to bring home for this or that zoo. The on-board routine was always the same. One trainee would be rostered as the aircraft navigator for each leg and he would come under the direct supervision of one of the two staff navigation instructors. The remaining students would be seated at suitably instrument-equipped tables, an equal number each side, in the rear of the aircraft. Their duty was to use all available aids, visual, radio and astronomical and monitor the work of the chap up front, making their own decisions as to corrective action when needed but, of course, not applying them.

Keeping check on this motley bunch was a permanent headache, but somehow or the other, we all managed it and in fact this programme proved a great success.

I shall not forget the one occasion when my fellow instructor was taken ill in Singapore and I had to operate the service home caring for the operating navigator and the remainder in the rear. This earned me a commendation from above, but I am quite sure also contributed to my premature grey hairs and baldness.

Although the York had Rolls-Royce Merlin engines, it was not a pressurised aircraft and certainly had no interior fuselage padding to deaden noise, so from start to finish one had to adjust to the deafening roar of those four noisy power plants. It was intriguing to watch the double loading doors on this ageing aeroplane, whilst moving on the ground, as they could be seen moving quite independently as if the fuselage was warping and thus they were best forgotten.

I was never quite sure which of our various loads gave me greatest cause for concern, engines or animals. Looking at a giant engine, on a block mounting and strapped to lashing points by metal cables, one had to avoid any thoughts of what might happen in the event of a crash or some form of emergency landing. I had little doubt that in such a case, inertia would have seen this mass of metal hurtle out through the flight deck taking the crew with it, but fortunately this never happened.

After a few months of operating 'animal' flights and in spite of disinfecting procedures, the aircraft literally stank and crews were given a special cleaning allowance in order to keep their uniforms in wearable and healthy condition. Flights rostered to operate to and from Calcutta or Bangkok were the least popular as they usually involved the carriage of animals or birds.

From Calcutta, we uplifted birds by the thousand. Normally they were minute finches, sprayed with various coloured dyes and housed in small bamboo cages, hundreds to a cage, so that even the cages picked up the stain from the mainly red and yellow colour of the dyes. The noise and dust were almost unbearable, to the extent that our only wish was to get off the aircraft as fast as humanly possible.

It was almost the same with monkeys, mainly Rhesus type I think. They too were packed into similar cages, poor pathetic little creatures, already frightened out of their wits once loaded on board, but in the air with the aircraft noise and the squeals of their companions, it was sometimes awful to see and hear. Fortunately, in due course, BOAC hired animal handlers to operate on these flights and so thereafter all creatures were properly fed and watered, and off-loaded when a night stop was made.

Larger animals were always a problem both from the point of view of onloading and care, and I noted that the animal handlers carried humane killers and devices to sedate where necessary.

We did however manage to derive some amusement from all of this, as in the classic case where the Captain was asked to hold back on his engine start-up procedures while we tried to get all the birds airborne in their cages, so that theoretically we would lighten the load for take-off. Believe that if you dare.

On another occasion we picked up a black panther and his crate was placed in the rear of the aircraft to avoid possible in-flight problems. The master compass unit on the York aircraft was sited behind a small door in the tail unit, and it was the navigator's duty to extract a reading before take-off and then compare this reading with the flight deck indicators. On this occasion, and fully aware of the possible outcome, we asked a particularly pompous and troublesome student to go aft and take the reading.

Off he proudly set, watched closely by those in the know and of course, of necessity, he had to step over the animal's crate which was resting across the fuselage. As he set foot on top of the crate and lifted himself up, the creature with a hiss and a mighty roar, hit the roof of the cage. I've seen fear in my time, but this was a rewarding sight to behold. Our man screamed, hurled himself forward into the compass compartment and crouched there hurling abuse at all and sundry. There was no way that he was going to recross that crate and it was not until our animal handler placed a thick blanket over the bars that he was induced to return, and then only by squeezing between the solid end of the crate and the fuselage.

And then there was the dead tiger. We were on-loading animals at Bangkok, when one of the crew noticed that whilst all of the others were snarling, growling or generally misbehaving, a tiger, and a large one at that, appeared to be sprawled lifelessly on the bottom of his cage. The Captain beckoned the local agent and asked for an explanation. 'Just sleeping Sahib, very tired, long journey from up country,' was the response as he waved to the loaders to go ahead. 'Hang on matey,' replied the Captain, 'when tigers sleep they still breathe and this one isn't'.

There then followed one of the finest performances I have ever seen, when the agent offered every excuse possible to explain why the supposedly sleeping tiger was not breathing, to the accompaniment of much hand wringing, pleading, and tears, but all to no avail. The beast was well and truly dead and had probably been so long before it had arrived at our aircraft. It gave us much cause for amusement, but had this agent succeeded in his deceit it would have proved costly to BOAC I'm sure.

There are numerous other anecdotes involving these flights but enough is enough, although I will mention in closing that there is nothing more disconcerting on a flight deck than to find the crew door suddenly thrust open and a number of small very lively birds tossed inside. I leave you to figure out why and to contemplate the end result. Be not shocked, we were not operating passenger-carrying flights and if it were not for these light-hearted lapses, we too would have been behind bars or in padded cells.

Anyway, somehow or other we managed to cope with the various problems and there is no doubt that, livestock apart, excellent navigational training was derived from these flights.

It was during this phase of route training and because the York freighter aircraft was on call to hasten urgent replacements to almost anywhere, that I found myself once more flying over strange territory, this time on the direct route to West Africa.

In 1953 on New Year's Eve, of all days, a crew, plus instructors and pupils were hastily assembled to operate 'Nan Sugar' out to Lagos. The actual aircraft registration was G-AGNS, but using the old style aviator's phonetical alphabet, the last two letters were given as 'Nan Sugar'. To anyone who had the misfortune to fly the Avro York in those far-off days, one only had to refer to 'Nan Sugar' and it immediately conjured up a vision of stench and noise.

So off we set on the longish haul to Tripoli, calling thankfully at Rome to top up with fuel on the way. Not that we were able to venture beyond the airfield at Rome, but at least we were able to make some worthwhile purchases in the duty free shop, during the transit. Then up into the air again, cracking the whip over our hard working pupils in the rear of the aircraft.

Quite a number of reliable radio transmitters had by now been established in and around the Mediterranean and these facilities, coupled with enforced astronomical work, gave students plenty to do and as they did not have the ultimate responsibility for navigating

An early conversion from military to civil livery.

Taxying up Southampton Water.

Disembarking passengers on the Zambesi.

The bar on board a Solent.

Forward section of the flight deck of a Hythe.

At moorings in Augusta harbour.

Flying boat over Victoria Falls.

On dry land for servicing.

In dock at Augusta.

The author attending mooring lines in the nose (ex gun turret) of a flying boat during a double engine change on the water at Basra.

The Avro York.

Argonaut refuelling at Nairobi.

The flight deck of a Stratocruiser.

The start of a long association with Boeing's big jets, this 707 is seen in the classic BOAC livery of white topsides, dark blue fuselage-stripe and tail, above polished aluminium undersides. The speedbird logo on the tail and 'BOAC' on the forward fuselage are picked out in gold.

the aircraft, they could go about their work in a relaxed manner and thereby gain confidence.

After landing at Castel Benito, as the airport at Tripoli was named, I thought back to wartime days when I had to bed down in a tent in a one-time vineyard nearby, whereas now we were hurtling down a good quality tarmac road, courtesy of a mad or drunken Libyan driver, on our way to the City and Port of Tripoli. Here we were accommodated in a recently refurbished top-quality hotel, where the rooms and service left nothing to be desired.

During the late evening, we assembled our students for a friendly and informal briefing, over a few beers, since the next stage, to be undertaken on the following night, would be a crossing of the Sahara Desert, down to Kano in Northern Nigeria, with no aids, other than the stars, so hard work and concentration would be the order of the day, or night.

On the following day we were able to rest and relax, indeed the Company arranged transport, so that in the earlier part of the day, we could visit a local beach and bathe in the sea, which was still comparatively warm. This was followed by a few hours in bed and then the duty call, setting us underway for a bath, kitting up, a meal and then another hair-raising ride which ensured that all senses were responsive by the time we reached our aircraft. Incidentally, on this occasion we had a couple of replacement engines on board and so there was not a lot of room to move between classroom and flight deck and even when one did so, there was a fair chance of tripping over the mass of cables used to secure the engines. Duly briefed, we were soon off into a moonless night sky, with myriads of stars already visible and just waiting for our sextants to warm up.

As always, in spite of the fact that the sun had long since set in the west, the initial noisy climb out included a succession of thuds and bumps as residual air turbulence threw us all over the sky, leaving some of the poor souls in the rear of the aircraft looking somewhat the worse for wear. This phase soon passed as we climbed into smoother air and then settled down at our cruising altitude. A quick radio call to Tripoli to report our height and position and then we were off over the vast stretch of featureless desert.

The students responded well to their briefing and were almost queuing up to get to the three sextants in the rear, whilst the pupil who had responsibility for the normal navigation was already hard at it.

Long before the days of high flying aircraft, equipped with

sophisticated onboard aids, crews used to fall back on some strange features as aids to establishing their position on this sector. The first was to rely upon the French Foreign Legion troops based at Gat or Djanet, both forts being on the border between Libya and Algeria, to stay awake and make their presence known. It was always very difficult to establish precisely when you were over one of these outposts, but quite often the Captain would switch on the aircraft landing lights and flash them on and off intermittently to show that we were looking out. In theory, the man sitting on top of the fort would then flash a light, thereby identifying himself and thus fixing our position for us. I suspect that on most flights which I undertook on that route, we were either off track, or the guard was using a candle, as only on one occasion did I see a light. In any case, when I did see the light, it was steady, but since there was virtually no life in that area other than at the forts, it did at least provide a reasonable check on position.

Another clue on progress stemmed from the advice given by some of the long-serving Captains who were weaned on practical rather than theoretical aids. My introduction to one of these particular aids, or clues, was on my first crossing of the Sahara when, without warning, and at a most unwelcome time, being in the middle of my astronomical observations, we were suddenly subjected to quite severe turbulence. Looking over his shoulder, the Captain in a knowledgable manner said 'That will be 19 North'. What he meant was that we had reached latitude 19 Degrees North, which since our track was predominantly in a southerly direction, gave a very useful check on progress. How did he know the latitude? The reason subsequently became clear for after studying the map at that latitude I noticed that the well marked Tange Mountain Ridge lies at right angles to the track and being high and rugged, it almost guarantees that overflying aircraft will be subject to the type of turbulence normally associated with mountain ranges. Just another wheeze, but a handy one to fall back on.

On into the night, with sextants working overtime, until the first signs of morning twilight appeared in the Eastern sky. One interesting point here. Readers may recall that a BOAC Hermes aircraft, flying this particular sector, crashed far off in the Western Sahara after running out of fuel. The navigational error which led to this accident is well-recorded and details do not matter here, but what is interesting is the usefulness of sighting morning twilight in the East.

On the Hermes flight, it is said, that it was thanks to an alert passenger who queried why the signs of first light in the east lay behind the aircraft, instead of to its left, which then led the crew to realise they were heading almost due west, by which time it was all too late and the outcome is history.

Shortly before dawn we were approaching the Nigerian border, where a very low-powered radio beacon had been sited at Zinder. The combination of low power and unreliable signals which occurred around dawn made this beacon practically useless as yet, but it gave some comfort to note that at least our instruments showed that the beacon lay somewhere roughly ahead. In due course, and after sunrise, the more powerful radio beacon at Kano was now being received loud and clear and it directed us on and in to this impressive capital of Northern Nigeria. Even in those comparatively early post-war days, the airfield was more than adequate for most needs, with a good long runway.

I always remained intrigued by the arrival signal given once an aeroplane was on the ground at Kano. This was provided by a huge swarthy Arab, of which tribe I never did discover. Wrapped in cream robes from head to toe, his face almost hidden by a huge turban and all of this perched on top of a massive camel, which seemed to curse, grunt and spit at the slightest provocation. The signal was given by a long blast on what appeared to be the local equivalent of a post horn and such was the resulting noise that all and sundry were left in no doubt as to the time and confirmation of arrival.

It was an interesting ride into Kano in a rickety old ex-RAF Bedford van, currently owned by the then West African Airways Company. The first stage of the journey was over little more than a dust-laden track, with scrub, some green and some brown, off to either side and with small rectangular mud huts popping up at random close by the track. Nearer to town, a tarmac-surfaced road made the ride much easier until we finally reached our night-stop accommodation. This was in a large comfortable guest-house owned by the Nigerian Railway Company, although, unfortunately, as we found out later, sleep was to be difficult to achieve under the huge mosquito nets with the mandatory electric fans rumbling and vibrating in the ceiling, as they did their best to circulate the humid air.

Kano had little to offer travellers, other than those with business interests, but just one visit to the old city was a must, even if only to see the racial mix, from all corners of the state including Tuareg in from the Sahara. A popular buy with crews in those days were the so-called 'Kano baskets'. These were multi-coloured circular baskets, presumably made from dried reed stems, each being topped by a huge flat removable lid. It was customary to buy a complete set starting with a basket of some two feet in diameter and then adding others on down through about six sizes, each one contained within its next largest partner, to the smallest, which was normally around eight inches across. Cheap they were, but by no means shoddy and even to this day, forty years on, my family have linen and needlework baskets from Kano in constant use and showing little signs of wear.

Apart from this one small shopping item, Kano had little else to offer and after a general get-together for a meal and a few beers in the evening, it was off to bed and what little sleep was possible.

Work the next day was hardly arduous, for all we had to cope with was a short flight down over the rapidly changing landscape, which switched from brown to rich green, into Lagos, unload our engines and then hot foot it back to Kano for another restless night. After which there followed the reverse procedure for the ride home, carrying anything and everything which the BOAC traffic and engineering staff en route decided had to be flown back to the United Kingdom.

Taken overall, there is no doubt that these flights and others further afield which were to follow later on, gave a good solid navigational foundation to those pilots, who for the present were reluctant navigators.

For the next two and a half years, my flying followed an unchanging pattern of short Dove flights to and from Shannon, followed by consolidation flights in the York flying classroom and then, finally, flights with individual students in the closing stage of their training, on Argonaut services almost anywhere.

Before this pattern did finally change, I was to be given a short unforecast break, and then only because of a last-minute problem.

In late 1955, BOAC had commenced operations using the Lockheed Constellation aircraft, which had previously been confined to North Atlantic routes, through to Australia, and with hardly time to wind my watch I was informed that due to crew sickness, I would be required to operate on one of these services through to Sydney.

I was given a very quick briefing on the flight planning and operating techniques and before I had time to consider possible problems, I was on my way.

This particular Lockheed Constellation aeroplane fell into the

100

mid-power range of this type. It was equipped with Wright Cyclone engines and was categorised as the Lockheed 749A. It had been preceded by the 049 series, and was succeeded by the larger and more powerful 1049 series – a very noisy machine, known affectionately by some as the Vibromaster.

To say that some of the Captains operating these aircraft were martinets would be an understatement. Accustomed to all the authority and glamour assumed by those who had for years operated BOAC's prestige route across the North Atlantic, they tended to treat all others as mere mortals.

I recall that on this particular flight, I was given a full scale dressing down, for daring to appear at briefing, in tropical temperatures at Darwin, with my shirt sleeves rolled up. Such was the standard of dress required of crews! On reflection, I reckon that perhaps this was not a bad thing after all. But perhaps the matter of discipline in dress, could have been handled a little more tactfully on this occasion. However, I took great delight in seeing that somewhat pompous Captain taken down a peg or two when we moved on from our pre-dawn briefing at Darwin, to partake of breakfast.

In those early days, the crew dining room at Darwin, in the Northern Territory of Australia, was no more than a canteen and on this occasion we all sat patiently and innocently at the kitchen-style table, awaiting service. This came in an unexpected way, when a large serving hatch was suddenly slammed open and a seemingly four ton, bare chested, craggy faced, Australian leaned through and said in a challenging manner 'What'll it be cobbers, steak or pork chops with your fried eggs'. With all the authority and majesty that he could summon, and after we had all timidly said yes to one or other of the offers of meat, our leader said 'I think I'll have scrambled eggs with a few slices of cold ham'. The reply was quite clear 'Like hell you will mate, you'll have chop or steak like yer cobbers, so what's it to be then'?

There was nothing he could do or say in answer to that offer and for our part it was difficult to stifle our chuckles. That's life for you, there seems to be compensation around when it is really needed.

Anyway this one-off trip to Australia provided a pleasant interlude and enabled me to see how the other half lived.

CHAPTER 8

MOVING FURTHER UP MARKET

V ery slowly BOAC were making significant changes to their route structures. New aircraft types were being introduced and some of the older types were then taken off prestige routes to become workhorses on other routes.

On the North Atlantic, the Douglas DC-7C had taken over from the giant Boeing Stratocruiser, the latter being relegated to West African routes, whilst lurking in the wings were the first of BOAC's giant Boeing jets, the 707s, waiting to be proved and slotted into flights from the United Kingdom to America and Canada.

Of course the ill-fated de Havilland Comet was operating regular flights to the Near and Far East and South Africa at this time, but its North Atlantic flights, such as they were, were badly affected by fuel limitations which often necessitated en route landings, when the 707 was able to fly right through with no such requirement.

In addition an early version of that superb aircraft, the Bristol Britannia, or Whispering Giant as it was known, was commencing its working life on the Eastern routes. This turbo-propellor aeroplane was a remarkable step forward. Powered by the Bristol Proteus engine it added a new dimension to our route operations, in that our ears were no longer subjected to the roar of piston engines and the additional power, particularly at hot and high altitude airfields, was a further bonus.

As far as I was concerned, one spin-off effect was that the consolidation flights made by our students were now to be conducted on these newer aeroplanes, hence I and my fellow tutors had to attend short ground courses and update our knowledge of planning and procedures.

Unfortunately, the early Britannia aircraft, the so-called 102 version, was plagued by engine icing problems which caused far too many in-flight incidents for safety, hence this machine was temporarily withdrawn from service whilst the experts attempted to solve the problem. Ice was apparently forming, or accumulating, in an intake bend on the inlet side of the engines, leading to what was effectively a flame-out. I won't bother readers with technicalities. Suffice it to say, as has often been described, we had a huge fire burning in a tin can in each engine and this kept going out! A solution of sorts was found by fitting 'glo plugs' to the engines thereby providing an automatic relight system.

I was on the outside of these problems until out of the blue, and certainly at very short notice, I became deeply involved and consequently learned at first hand what it was like to experience the effect of this strange engine behaviour in flight. I had already been taught the new techniques involved in flight planning for this aircraft and had reached the stage when I was able to conduct short courses of instruction myself. At this time, the Britannia 102 had been taken off route flying while the boffins did their thing, although the 'glo plug' solution had by now been put in hand.

The Suez Crisis came to a head in the first week of November and there was an immediate demand for troops to be flown out to Aden in large numbers. The RAF could not cope with the overall demand and thus BOAC were hauled in to help. Obviously, aircraft could not be taken off scheduled services, so where could the Corporation turn to, but the grounded Britannia fleet?

I have no doubt that had the passengers not been unfortunate soldiers, who dare not complain anyway, this aircraft would not have been used: but it was, and just as unfortunately for me, I happened to be close by the manager's office when the call came through.

I was taken in like a lamb to the slaughter when the manager innocently, or so it seemed, remarked to me 'You are pretty well up on Britannia flight planning aren't you'. I could hardly deny what was a fact and his follow up statement was to the effect that I would have to form part of one of a number of crews, due to depart on the following morning, conveying hundreds of troops to Aden.

Since the Britannia fleet had been temporarily disbanded and the crew members dispersed, it was a matter of grabbing the first of those suitably qualified staff who happened to be around. Meanwhile, ground engineers were already working overtime to have the aircraft ready for the following morning. So bad was the situation that BOAC had to borrow one navigator from the RAF unit at Lyneham, where they were still operating the Britannia in a military configuration.

There was much frantic to-ing and fro-ing in our headquarters building, the major problem being the selection of routes which would have to be flown. With troops on board, there was no question of landing at civil airports and finally, in conjunction with Government departments and with much help from other countries, it was decided that we would operate via Algiers, Kano and Nairobi and thence up to Aden.

Then came the crunch – since there was no accommodation en route to cope with such a load, we would all have to operate right through to Nairobi without a break. The things one does for one's country, although of course we had no option.

In the rush and excitement of preparation, the icing problem had been forgotten, but it soon came to the fore, once we got underway.

We left London at a very early hour and the climb to cruising altitude in this powerful machine was pretty rapid, but the fun started once we had settled down at our chosen height. We had flown in and out of layered cloud, which in the normal course of events would have created no problem, but not so now. One by one, and at quite irregular intervals, the engines began to misbehave, to be followed by a disconcerting thud as each relit. It was the unresolved icing problem rearing its ugly head, and from that point on, whether in or out of cloud, both pilots were on constant alert, presumably fearing a total shut-down.

I have no knowledge of the technicalities involved: all I know was that it was extremely disquieting to have one's routine constantly interrupted by cross calls from up front, such as 'No. 2 is going' followed by a relight thump and then all over again. Things did improve the further south we went, but even at higher air temperatures the overall problem still persisted, though to a lesser degree.

Transit refuelling stops at Algiers and Kano passed without problem and since our passengers were not given time to disembark, the atmosphere became a little high in the aircraft cabin, to say the least.

The flight from Kano to Nairobi was of great interest to me, since it was over unknown territory, mainly the Congo, and it was thus devoid of any powerful radio aids to help us on our way. Map-reading was out of the question since this was to be a moonless night flight and in any case the maps provided were of little use other than where the major river patterns appeared. So it would be sextant work all the way, interrupted, just as I had anticipated, by engine 'bumps' when least expected.

Mind you, we had all become somewhat accustomed to this worrying engine behaviour by now and the one redeeming feature was that the mighty Proteus engines continued rotating regardless.

Our track took us to the north of the great sweep of the mighty Congo River and I do recall, in the thick of night, tuning the radio compass receiver in to a radio beacon sighted at Bangui, on the River Ubangi, a branch of the Congo, more out of interest than for any other reason, only to find to my surprise a strong signal emanating from down below. Star observations had given good results thus far, but it was comforting to find that the radio beacon at Bangui confirmed we were on, or pretty close to, our desired track.

With no moon above and an inky blackness below, there was no point in straining one's eyes to seek out visual checkpoints, and in any case, as I have already observed, the maps for that region were not particularly detailed. However, I was intrigued to observe a strange orange glow from the ground far ahead, which as we came closer, appeared as crescent-shaped clusters of bright lights, glowing intermittently with red, yellow and orange light. This strange phenomenon stretched far off to the left and right as we closed with it, at which point the penny dropped when I recalled seeing a similar sight in the Southern Sudan many years before. What we were now looking at was a massive collection of disconnected bush fires raging below, being driven forward by the wind and consequently burning in giant curved lines. It was an awe-inspiring sight and looking closer one could see the rise and fall of the light as presumably the flames consumed trees, in their relentless path forward. Like so many strange sights in aviation one moved slowly towards it but then suddenly it passed below and was gone.

Fortunately for us the Inter-Tropical Front, which with small breaks, girdles the earth, was way off to the south, though on the far horizon intermittent yellow flashes indicated its associated thunderstorm activity.

We plodded on through the night and the early signs of morning twilight raised spirits somewhat as we would soon have sight of the ground and hopefully confirmation of the results of my sextant observations. In the event, dawn revealed an almost unending bank of cloud below, although first radio contact with Nairobi advised us that the weather there was good.

The first rewarding sight, was not of a recognisable landmark below, but far off to the south, as we neared the great Lake Victoria, were the jagged peaks of the Ruwenzori Range, on the border between Uganda and the Congo. I have a feeling that because of their appearance this range of mountains was known as the Mountains of the Moon but, right or wrong, they remained a sight which I will never forget. Stark peaks jutting out from cloud like huge stalagmites, the highest I believe reaching over 16,000 feet above sea level.

Cloud began to break up approaching Lake Victoria and after a hard day and night's work, it was a pleasure to look down at the lakeshore, far below, and follow it eastwards from Entebbe until reaching its eastern boundary, by which time our radio compass had locked firmly on to the powerful radio beacon at Nairobi and we commenced the long descent into the Capital.

For reasons which I cannot remember, we had to remain at Nairobi for three days before finally nipping up to Aden to complete the flight, and a day or so later we returned home with an almost empty aircraft. I say almost because anybody or anything waiting to be transported back to the United Kingdom, made full use of this flight, although some of our passengers were not all that happy when they discovered the, as yet unmentioned, engine noises. Since we were now a non-military flight, we were able to call at Entebbe on the way home, but still had to make the trans-Congo flight back to Kano, thence to London via Tripoli.

CHAPTER 9

RETURN TO ERIN'S ISLE

The Suez incident behind us, it was back to a routine training programme again, but with a further step up in recruitment, the pattern had now changed slightly.

I spent far more time in the recently opened Ground Training Centre, sited on the Eastern Perimeter of Heathrow, and close to all the aviation activities, where noise and the sight of aeroplanes added more realism and urgency to our training programmes.

For my part, I had been appointed to teach subjects which formed part of the Flight Navigator's licence syllabus, with the emphasis on flight planning, navigation plotting and astronomical work. Whilst these subjects were certainly more practical than, say, magnetism or radio, they still required a good sound knowledge of principles and theory, which included, as an example, spherical trigonometry.

These requirements inevitably led to much complaining from the usual bunch of agitators, but faced with the prospect of no examination passes, no licence, no job, the effect was remarkable.

With hindsight, I reckon that we could have dealt with some of our complainants in a more considerate manner. As an example, I remember one ex-Navy pilot, who incessantly argued that when flying busy routes with more than adequate radio navigational aid coverage most of our basic navigation procedures could be considered as unnecessary. He was duly squashed by the purists, but it is worthy of note that this man went on to become a senior Concorde pilot, wrote a book on this aircraft and, not many years later, the longstanding route procedures were dropped in favour of radio-backed systems, just as he had dared to suggest.

I suppose our time was split evenly, with probably a week in ground school, followed by another of continuous flights by day and night, to and from Shannon.

Shortly before Government examinations were required, students were rostered for normal route flights, accompanied by one of our

107

team. This was simply to step up the pace and iron out any residual bugs in their practical work.

Incidentally, part of the licence qualification requirement was a specific number of operational flying hours, rounded off with a flight test carried out on a normal passenger-carrying sector or sectors. For this purpose, we instructors had been appointed as Government Aviation Examiners.

During our first year of involvement in this type of mixed work, BOAC had begun to withdraw the mighty Boeing Stratocruiser from the North Atlantic route and replaced it with the faster, more modern Douglas DC-7 aircraft. However with some useful life remaining, they decided to use the 'Strat', on flights to West Africa.

Since much of our student continuation training included flights to that part of the world, it now became necessary for us to undertake a short course of training in the planning and operating techniques of this giant Boeing aircraft. That completed, we were then in a position to escort our young men on Stratocruiser flights to Nigeria. A great improvement on the Argonaut, the Boeing being quieter and more powerful and with a longstanding and proven good safety record.

In November 1957 I found myself, with one of our lambs, briefed and ready to depart for Lagos via Rome and Kano, on Boeing G-ANTZ christened *Cordelia*. Elated at the thought of modern comforts on this aircraft I had forgotten one most important point which was soon brought home very forcibly to me.

The Stratocruiser crew were all ex-North Atlantic Gods, *La Crème de la Crème*, who had been yanked from heaven to operate on this smelly subtropical route. Although I had met them formally at briefing, I was totally unprepared for the flight deck reception.

I found the Captain already seated in the massive pilot's chair where he had donned a brightly coloured crew, or 'mission', cap with a minute boom microphone swinging from some sort of head attachment. He was yelling orders to the flight engineer who sat at the huge instrument-covered console, busy tapping, switching and swearing all at the same time. Here was another character indeed, weighing around sixteen stone I guess, he was wearing some sort of bomber jacket, a similar crew cap to that worn by the Captain, but jammed in the corner of his mouth was a massive plastic cigar holder crammed into which was an equally large cigar, unlit of course.

The conversation, if that was the correct description for the verbal crossfire, was carried out at a volume equivalent to about 110 decibels, and completely ignored the arrival of other crew members on to the flight deck. I deduced later that this conversation had something to do with take-off procedures wherein water injection was a factor.

The engineer's instrument panel had me completely baffled, although in due time I was given a run down on the main components. That which intrigued me most was the engine analyser, which enabled the flight engineer to scan effectively, amongst other things, the ignition system of each engine whilst in flight and to detect faults even down to, say, identifying a dud sparking plug. This was a most useful instrument as, after flight, it enabled the flight crew to direct ground engineers straight to probable fault areas and thus to take remedial action without the need for exploratory engine running.

The 'mission men' from the North Atlantic, certainly in the early days of West African operations, seemed to live in a past age of their own, acknowledging solely their own kind. There seemed to be constant battles between pilot and engineer as to who should control and handle the throttles and if one set them up for, say, cruising conditions, as soon as his hand was removed another would slide in to make minor adjustments. Not that they were necessary but status seemed to be all important – most amusing.

The navigator and radio officer positions on this aircraft tended to be out of the way, almost as if set up as an afterthought, but to be fair, they, and the aircraft, turned out to be comfortable, quiet and reliable.

Having overcome the initial shock, and adjusted to the ways of these 'moon men', the flight down to West Africa followed the accustomed routine, although of course it was faster than before, and once settled into the in-flight routine, I and my student could remain in our little patch ready to supply all necessary information as and when required.

In truth, as time progressed, these North Atlantic gods came down off their pedestals and overcame the enforced tolerance to the extent that we all grew to like each other, almost without exception.

One plus point for some of us stemmed from the fact that a large number of Stratocruiser people had been seconded to the North Atlantic routes during the war, whereas most of our group were ex-wartime RAF with a tale or two to tell. We often used this background to put down our North Atlantic friends and out of this situation grew mutual respect and excellent working relationships.

The arrival at Lagos provided another shock, or rather a pleasant surprise for me, when as I was about to leave the flight deck, the passengers having already disembarked, I was asked to hang on for a moment.

I dutifully obeyed and a short moment later, the senior steward stepped on to the flight deck with a tray of champagne cocktails. Apparently just to round off the flight and wind us down ready for a good night's rest. I reckon that those North Atlantic boys had it made, and goodness knows what else went on, on those one-time prestige flights.

In the months which followed, life again became a mix of all aspects of navigation training. The initial flights continued, using the de Havilland Dove, with an additional bonus since we were now able to use the Channel Islands as an optional destination to Shannon. An interesting change of scenery, and still with the attraction of duty-free goods.

In addition, and presumably to reduce training costs, it was decided to send the York flying classroom to Gibraltar, from which point it would make a series of night flights out over the Mediterranean, providing excellent opportunities for astronomical work, and from a purely selfish point of view, a delightful base at the Rock Hotel where food and drink were cheap and plentiful.

This was one of the few York training exercises which had a queue of willing volunteers standing by at all times. In mid-1959, another trough appeared in the training progress graph and so, once more, my colleagues and I were ordered to return to regular route flying. As an added bonus, my earlier Britannia experience now stood me in good stead and I was moved, on a temporary basis, to the unit operating the more advanced model which had now arrived, namely the Britannia B312, a larger and superior version.

Fortunately at long last I was now to venture westwards across the North Atlantic.

Chapter 10

Over the Pond

In those days, a North Atlantic crossing to the United States or Canada involved a certain amount of complex planning. Part of the reason was the somewhat limited range of some of the aeroplanes, when set against the North Atlantic weather.

Firstly, as so frequently happened, with a weather depression sitting out in mid-Ocean, the wind flow pattern at most heights was predominantly westerly, and since in jet streams at our operating altitude the wind speed could reach 150 knots or more, routes had to be chosen with great care. It was almost for sure that head winds aloft would preclude us from using the shortest direct route, known as the Great Circle, and lead us to use a more northerly track.

If you study the wind flow pattern around a surface depression you will note that the circulation in the top right quadrant is from the east and flows in a westerly direction, and although this did not always apply precisely at our cruising heights, it did at least mean that we could avoid headwinds by flying on a more northerly track.

This invariably meant that we would have to head up to Prestwick, in Ayrshire, and then off towards the southern tip of Greenland, after which we could head in a direction south of west to pass over either the Goose Airport in Labrador, or Gander in Newfoundland, thence on down to Montreal, Toronto, Boston or New York, as required.

The airfields at Goose and Gander were extremely useful to us for a variety of reasons. As an example, quite often in winter, we would leave London without sufficient fuel to reach, say, New York with the legally required reserves of fuel, due mainly to strong head winds. For this reason, we would declare Goose or Gander as our destination, and as a consequence we then had sufficient fuel to depart and satisfy the safety legislation. However, in flight, we would keep a very careful eye on progress, using an in-flight fuel and distance graph known as a 'Howgozit', and if all went well, it was possible, more often than not, to conserve a little fuel and replan an onward flight from Goose or Gander, to our destination without landing to refuel.

This was not an unsafe practice, but merely a means of determining a revised reserve fuel requirement for arrival at destination. To explain: it was usual, apart from other considerations, to add a fixed percentage of the fuel required to fly from departure to destination, as a safety factor. This could be a sizeable amount of fuel, but if we replanned in flight, taking the same percentage of fuel between say Gander and New York it produced a significant reduction in the reserve requirement, when compared with that for London to New York, and thus enabled us to press on. All legitimate and all safe.

Another important factor adding to planning complexity was that the winter weather in Canada and the United States can spring many surprises at short notice and it was not uncommon, having left London with a forecast of possible snow showers at the other end, to discover in mid-Atlantic that the destination weather had gone down below permitted landing limits, often in blizzard conditions.

It was in such conditions that aircraft from all over would flock to those two huge maritime airfields – Goose and Gander – which had proved life savers to many thousands of flight crew. Mind you, they too often closed down due to bad weather, invariably heavy snow, and under such circumstances we had a major decision to make as to whether to go on to destination alternative airfields, way ahead, or return to London.

Pre-flight planning to avoid head winds and possibly gain advantage from following winds at higher altitudes, could be quite an involved process and included a theoretical analysis of all available weather charts.

It was possible, by use of simple template measurements, graphs and mathematical tables to determine what were known as wind component values for various stages of the optional routes. The wind component merely indicated the likely increase or reduction in ground speed, produced by given wind flow situations and was of great value in planning.

On my first North Atlantic flight on the larger Britannia aircraft, we ran into the usual problem of head winds and a decision was made before departure, to drop into Gander en route and top up with fuel, before proceeding on to New York, our ultimate destination being Jamaica via Bermuda. My flying log-book records that we departed from London just before midnight, for the long haul on the northerly route, destined to take around eight and a half hours.

The weather forecast, even at our planned moderately high altitude was such that astronomical observations would not be possible. Fortunately for us, we had two alternative radio aids available, the Consol system and the Loran long-range navigation equipment.

The Consol system required the navigator to tune into any one of three radio stations, positioned in Northern France, Northern Ireland and at Nantucket in the USA and then count the number of morse dots and dashes which were to be heard. These always totalled 60, but the number of each type heard varied with the position of the aircraft in relation to the ground transmitter. These various combinations of dots and dashes were printed on to a special chart and all that the navigator had to do was to find the appropriate combination which then indicated the aircraft bearing from the station. A most useful line of position, but due to the vagaries and limitations of this type of radio signal, this facility fast faded as one drew further away from land.

Loran was a different and far more reliable system. Transmitting stations were widely spaced along our routes giving almost complete radio coverage. A cathode-ray tube was used by the navigator and signals from the various stations appeared on this screen as conventional radar blips. By comparing the relative position of pairs of blips on the screen, a mathematical value was determined for each difference and this value appeared as a position line on a plotting chart. Unlike the Consol system, Loran enabled the navigator to take a number of readings from each ground station group, or chains as they were known, at close intervals and thereby obtain pretty accurate position fixes.

Like most radio aids, this system suffered from the usual problems, in that it had limited range at low altitudes and was subject to interference, particularly from static electricity associated with rain, or other forms of precipitation. Interference manifested itself as a mass of so called 'grass' on the screen, but most of us became past masters at the art of peering into this mass and identifying the required signals.

Most of the northerly routes just tipped the southernmost point of Greenland, where at King Christian Island, a radio beacon had been positioned, a more than welcome aid. On a couple of occasions only did I actually fly over mainland Greenland where the mass of rock and ice below looked desolate and most uninviting.

It is interesting to note that on the south-western coast of Greenland an airfield had been set up by the Americans many years previously in association with wartime ferry flights to the European war zone. This field was positioned at the end of a long inlet bordered by high ground and once committed and headed in towards the field, you were in a 'no return' situation since there was insufficient room to make a turn to the left or right. Fortunately this bolt-hole was quite unsuitable for large aircraft and from the many stories I had heard of hazardous approaches in the past, that suited me just fine.

The then current schedules to America meant that we often experienced morning twilight somewhere between Greenland and Labrador and it was on one such occasion that I had my first site of icebergs.

The Britannia aircraft had been fitted with weather radar equipment, and by tilting the forward scanner it was possible to pick up large surface masses, most useful when approaching a well-defined coastline. On this occasion, what should have been a clear screen, since we were over the sea, did in fact show an odd blip or two. I was very quickly put into the picture by the more experienced pilots and guided by them I looked ahead and there saw several giant masses of ice below, the icebergs so dreaded by mariners. From the air, and with clear seas, the ice appeared to be surrounded by a bright green base, which in fact is the submerged, and largest portion of the berg, disappearing down into the depths of the ocean. A most impressive, awe-inspiring and indeed frightening sight.

Our approach to Canada or the States in those days was carefully monitored, and the control boundaries were marked at intervals by so-called 'fish' points, simply because each point was named after a fish. One had to be very accurate in navigation procedures to ensure arriving precisely over the nominated entry point and equally important to be there at the estimated time which you had previously advised. Woe betide you if you failed to do so and certainly a radar monitoring system was in operation to keep a watchful eye from down below.

I had heard talk that aircraft might be scrambled to intercept if you were found to be in breach, but I never met anyone who had experienced this action and I suspect that it was just a scare story to keep us on our toes.

What was certain was that if an aircraft did abuse procedures by missing one of these check points, a violation was filed against the Company and a fairly hefty financial penalty ensued. If the aircraft was scheduled to overfly without refuelling then, once over one or other of the two maritime airports, Goose or Gander, it was slotted into the airways system, where air traffic control officers took over and dictated the route, height and at times even the speed.

At this point the navigator could relax, since his main task had been completed, although he was expected to keep an eye on progress and to revise the estimated arrival time if necessary, and even to calculate any change in remaining fuel requirements. That apart, one could sit back, and if weather conditions permitted, enjoy the changing scenery below.

Northerly airway routes tended to converge over Seven Islands, on the northern shore of the St Lawrence Seaway, and then diverge, depending on the destination. If flying on to Montreal or Toronto, the route followed the St Lawrence, but if bound for New York or Boston the airway headed in a southerly direction across the State of Maine.

Western Labrador and Newfoundland, once away from the coast, seemed to consist of thousands upon thousands of small lakes, swamps and forests with no sign of a road or track for hundreds of miles, a true wilderness. Inevitably, as one moved south-westwards, signs of civilisation began to creep in until finally the scene below returned to what, to someone used to flying over Europe, became normal and civilised.

One of the grandest sights in this part of the world is the forest land below seen during autumn when the maple leaves turn to various shades of red and brown and when these mix with evergreen conifers they make the earth below resemble some giant Persian Carpet. Money could not buy a picture like that, and to the aviator it is all there for free.

As the numerous airways converge at destination points, life becomes very hectic. Taking New York as an example, one generally knew well in advance, particularly if the weather was at all suspect, that there would be a delay in approach and landing and in the run in over Long Island a number of so-called holding points had been established, where aircraft were stacked at various levels, patiently circling until given the order to descend and finally to commence an approach to land.

A frequent problem at New York stemmed from the fact that there were three airfields in the vicinity and many light aircraft using them often failed to observe standard procedures, so that the big boys were left sitting up aloft whilst controllers struggled to direct a small private aeroplane through the other traffic and down on to *terra firma*.

Digressing for a moment, an experience, though not for the faint-hearted or those of a nervous disposition, was to arrive over New York, by day or night, at a peak operating time and as so often happened, during a snow storm.

The radio telephony channels would be choked up with frustrated pilots sitting at the back end of a long queue at the end of the runway struggling to obtain take-off clearance. Meanwhile up aloft equally irate incoming crews would be calling for priority approaches due to fuel shortage after a long Atlantic crossing. So bad was the situation at times that jet aircraft, which had been cleared to start engines and move to the runway, would have to return in order to top up with fuel.

Delays of the order of 40 minutes were not unusual and engines running for 40 minutes on the ground burn up a tremendous amount of fuel. One could not sit and wait until later before starting up, since this meant losing a place in the take-off queue. Frustrating is hardly the word for it.

For those awaiting approach clearance many were the ruses used to jump the landing queue. A worried call from a four-engined jet Captain to say that an engine was misbehaving or that fuel was getting short, did work for a while but eventually controllers became wise, even though some cases were genuine, and they tended to advise aircraft to divert to a less congested airfield while they could.

When it comes to slick radio telephony procedures there is no one to compete with the Americans. They are highly efficient, quick to respond and to me, always seemed unflappable. They also had a great sense of humour, far removed from the gentlemanly formality of our own British controllers. I well remember a departure from New York on the eve of Princess Margaret's wedding, an event far removed from our minds as we listened to the mass of departure instructions coming from the American controller, but as he finished, he added 'Oh, Yeah, and don't forget to give our love to the Princess'.

However, returning to the hectic arrival scene, there is the classic story of a Boeing 707 pilot who was given a priority approach, as he was in trouble and flying on three engines. He was interrupted by a charter aircraft pilot, who asked to be brought in ahead since he was flying on two engines. You've guessed it, he was given number one spot for landing and as he touched down the controller awoke to the fact that it was a Cessna aircraft, which only had two engines anyway, so he did not lie, he obtained his priority and landed in poor weather conditions, under normal power.

However, I have jumped way ahead of myself, since on this occasion, having landed at Gander, after due clearance, we settled on to the long runway and taxied in to join many other aircraft, all busy topping up their fuel supplies before pressing on westwards.

Because of its unique position, staff at Gander were quite used to handling large numbers of aircraft, but since this was strictly a transit airfield, the facilities for passengers and crew were very limited. The terminal building was modern enough, but few passengers disembarked at this spot since there was nothing thereabouts to attract stopover travellers although I understand that shooting and fishing were the finest to be found anywhere. It was always interesting, in winter, and whilst waiting to refuel, to see how other crews handled their take-off under extreme snow and ice conditions.

Very often an aircraft would be seen to move slowly down the runway at the start of its take-off run, but as it gathered speed, clouds of snow would be sent showering into the air obscuring the rear end and leaving a vertical white blanket behind, which slowly drifted and subsided after the aeroplane had departed.

Not always a comforting sight, as we would inevitably have to follow the same procedure shortly after. There was no real danger in operating under such conditions, but obviously special techniques were needed and weight limitations had to be applied, particularly for landing.

A coffee and sandwich and we were up and away to join the crowded airway to New York, where after the usual period of holding over Long Island, we were duly slotted in for landing.

To me, a new boy to this route, everything seemed to be well organised both in the air and on the ground as we moved from one phase to another. A quick clearance through the special crew Customs section and on to the Company office where we were handed our cash allowance to cover subsistence whilst staying in the Big Apple.

Then on to the largest limousine I had ever seen, for the run into town. The traffic build-up as we approached Manhattan was tremendous and left one wondering how we would ever make it to the hotel, but the hundreds of vehicles eased forward, albeit with impatient drivers, until we finally entered the tunnel under the East River where things speeded up a little. It always amused me to see New York's 'finest' patrolling a form of catwalk on the side of the tunnel and frantically waving their night sticks to urge drivers on. As if anyone wanted to delay after the dreadful traffic jam approaching the Tunnel.

BOAC crews were accommodated in good hotels in central Manhattan, although, for a time, pilots were sent to one hotel and the remainder of the crew to another.

If I recall correctly, for the many subsequent stopovers which I enjoyed in New York, the crews stayed in one of two hotels on Lexington Avenue, by 45th Street, ideally placed for most of what New York had to offer.

There was so much to occupy our time in that city, that crews, somewhat unusually, would tend to split up and do their own thing. The exception to this practice involved a bar and delicatessen, both of which were somewhere behind the hotel, on 3rd Avenue, I think. This 'Deli' provided almost any type of fast food or drink that one could require and was very handy if a long westbound haul from London had left one too tired to consider going out to a restaurant on arrival.

My spelling may be suspect, but I know that I have the name of the bar right, when I say that it was 'Kulkin's'. For the life of me I don't know why it had been singled out by crews, apart from the fact that staff were friendly and it was close to the hotel but, always, the parting words, after checking into the hotel and entering the elevator on the way to one's room, were invariably 'See you in Kulkin's in half an hour'. So popular was this bar that rumour had it crew members were arranging for a tunnel to be built from the hotel to the bar so that in mid-winter, when snow lay really deep on the sidewalks, crews would not be denied their visit to this hostelry.

It is impossible to describe in detail everything which New York had to offer and, in any case, tastes varied so much that, other than shopping, crews found vastly different attractions to follow.

At that time and with economy in mind, a favourite eating house was Tad's steak bar. There were several of these eateries in the central area, the attraction being that one could have a steak, grilled to order, with a side salad for $1.99. Mind you, we did not confine our eating to Tad's and we patronised many of the fine specialist restaurants on Third Avenue where food was very costly, but extremely good.

For my part, I tended to walk most of the time during my days off, and being a creature of habit, I trod almost the same path each time. A slow walk along 42nd Street, past the cinemas and theatres and then up into Broadway and Times Square, which need no description. I usually popped into the famous Long Bar off Times Square where many of the brilliant Negro musicians performed either as part of an organised programme, or as I discovered later, on a casual basis if they happened to be around.

On a day of poor weather I would then complete the Square by heading back eastwards towards Park Lane, always calling at Korvettes on the way. This company, which no longer exists, operated a number of discount stores where goods always seemed to be of top quality and at that time crews concentrated on buying popular long playing records and portable garden furniture, the latter being quite easily transportable with our baggage. I invariably paid the almost mandatory visit to Grand Central Station, not so much to marvel at the hustle and bustle on the main concourse, but to view the famed giant Kodak coloured picture display, set high in the roof. This was unbelievably large, brilliantly coloured and highly detailed and the subject matter of the picture varied regularly from children through transport to beautiful panoramic views. Very difficult to adequately describe but suffice it to say that the quality and variety of subjects made such a visit a must for most of us.

If weather permitted, I would set off early and walk the length of Broadway, from Times Square down to the southernmost tip of Manhattan, at the Battery Point. One could sit alongside the water here and watch the world go by whilst giving aching feet a short respite. Then off to the east towards the Staten Island Ferry point, subsequently turning north through some of the most interesting sections of Manhattan.

One must remember that in the mid-50s, mugging was a rarity and it was possible to walk almost anywhere in complete freedom. I invariably arranged for my homebound journey to take me up through Motte Street in the centre of Chinatown, from which point, I would pick up Third Avenue, or thereabouts, and wander through the Jewish quarter. It was fascinating in this section of town to walk in and out of the hundreds of pawn shops and many were the bargains to be obtained thereabouts. A popular buy for crews were the Samsonite suitcases which retailed for no more than $10 or quite often less, depending on your bargaining prowess. Golf clubs could also be obtained for a song and they were good quality sets at that.

With so much of interest to occupy the time, I often arrived back at the hotel after dark, but safely, I am happy to say.

One could write a book, indeed many have, on all that New York has to offer. One thing is for sure and that is that once a visitor has done all the expected things, which at that time included a visit to the Rockefeller Center to watch the famed Rockettes dance, Central Park, Fifth Avenue, Greenwich Village and the great stores operated by Maceys and Gimbels, you had really only just begun to scratch the surface.

Walking was the only true way to see and enjoy this wonderful city and time and time again I stumbled upon famous streets and sights purely by chance, names which I then recalled from past Hollywood films. The weary traveller, in those days, could always fall back on the subway system, which was cheap and reliable.

I seem to remember that one of the ferry rides, possibly the Staten Island service, cost virtually nothing yet gave superb views of Manhattan on the way across. More costly, but far more rewarding, were the boat trips around Manhattan Island via the East and Hudson Rivers or the even more extensive cruise up the Hudson, towards West Point Academy.

Suffice it to say that when my visiting days were over, I felt certain that I had seen only a fraction of what New York had to offer.

However, to return to this, my maiden flight to the Caribbean. After our stopover, the next stage involved three shortish hops, mainly to cope with local holiday traffic. First, a flight down the east coast and across to Nassau, whence after the briefest of stops, since we did not require fuel, on to Bermuda.

Although on subsequent occasions I had the opportunity of overnight stops at Bermuda, I could never work up much enthusiasm for this island. That it was a rich man's paradise was beyond question, but for those living a normal existence it did seem to have limitations. In addition to this, although I accept that my visits were mainly out of season, I saw plenty of rain and on one occasion felt the fringe effects of a hurricane.

Anyway we were soon off to Jamaica, where we landed at the rapidly growing holiday resort of Montego Bay, to be accommodated at the famed Montego Bay Hotel.

These were early days for the Britannia services and consequently we had the best of everything the island had to offer and it was not until some years later that, although disembarking our passengers at 'Mo' Bay as it was affectionately known, we were then required to take our aircraft across the island to the airfield at the capital, Kingston, where surroundings and facilities were somewhat different to say the least.

Anyway, for the present, we were able to relax on the beach at Montego Bay and to soak up all that was on offer.

The return home came all too quickly, although the first day was hardly worth a mention since it consisted of a short hop up to Nassau, a rapid refuelling stop and then another couple of hours to Bermuda where we handed our aircraft over to a waiting crew, who would take it on to London.

Precisely 24 hours later, we took over an incoming aeroplane for the long ride home. On average, bearing in mind that prevailing winds were behind us, it still took nine hours or so for the mid-Atlantic crossing from Bermuda to London.

Once again this meant breaking new ground for me, and although there was some form of Loran coverage in mid-Atlantic, signals were often too weak to be useable and it was back to the dear old sextant again. Fortunately, the Britannia provided a very stable platform for taking star sights, hence much of the navigation on this crossing consisted solely of astronomical fixes.

I confess, whilst at Bermuda, that I did give a quick thought to the numerous stories of missing aircraft in that part of the world, in the so-called Bermuda Triangle, and it is a fact that there were mysterious disappearances. As to the reason, that had been the subject of speculation for many a year, but since ships have also gone missing, one must look for a common factor and that is presumed to be the magnetic compass. Enough said, and the theories are best left to specialists and story writers, although no one has produced anything resembling an acceptable answer yet.

Even after the many years of flying which now lie behind me, I often wonder what would happen in the event of a significant engine or equipment failure in mid-ocean, and these thoughts usually occurred whilst working on a chart which showed nothing but sea, with the welcoming coastlines folded underneath on its far edges.

I won't go into details of this crossing as the navigation was basically routine, but it was always comforting when Loran signals eventually started to appear strong and clear on the cathode-ray tube and the European radio beacons could be heard without inter-ference.

Our inbound route usually commenced at the Scilly Isles or Lundy island in the Bristol Channel and what a comforting sight it was to see them appear in the east at morning twilight. Then the all powerful Airway Air Traffic Controller at the London centre would take over and it was but a short time before we were on the ground, clearing Customs control and looking forward to a spell of relaxation at home.

I daresay, when one reels off stories of life at the delightful stopover points, that our job as aircrew seemed to be somewhat glamorous, but it was far from being so one-sided.

I could easily list a whole variety of incidents and accidents in the air, or on the ground, which analysis would probably show outweighed the fun side of things, particularly if you were a worrying type.

A reasonable break at home, during which time I was reintroduced to my children again and then into battle once more. My remark regarding the children may seem a little facetious but of course there were long spells of absence, during which my wife had to cope with their upbringing and the general running of our home, whilst I seemingly enjoyed myself at exotic places all over the world. Not really so, of course, because as faster and more efficient aircraft came along and passenger traffic demands grew, so the number of flights was stepped up and overseas stopover times reduced as a consequence. Long or short trips, there is no doubt that my long-suffering wife had a lot to contend with.

Following the Caribbean trip, I became involved once again in a mix of flights embracing the Far East and Central Africa until, in September 1959, I was ordered back to the Training Unit to take-up once more full-time ground tutoring work.

This involved imparting knowledge of the many theoretical subjects required for a Flight Navigator's Licence, to further groups of reluctant and unenthusiastic pilots, who, quite reasonably, just wanted to fly aeroplanes.

However, knowing that these hurdles had to be surmounted before they could eventually move on to their chosen profession, they knuckled under and invariably achieved excellent theoretical and practical results.

I had an unbroken run of six months dealing with these fine chaps, when, as so often happens, operational demands suddenly fell off and at fairly short notice I was returned to full-time flying duties yet again.

Chapter 11

Over the Pond Again

I n the Spring of 1960, although I did not realise it at that time, I was destined to settle down to North Atlantic flights on a regular basis until threats of a drastic cut in air crew numbers caused me to look hastily elsewhere, and as it so happened, discover another career of sorts, although still very much in aviation.

However, my initial move was to join the DC-7C flight which operated exclusively on the North Atlantic, to New York, Boston, Montreal and Toronto, so all the perks attached to that particular unit were soon to come my way.

Unfortunately, the DC-7C, powered by Wright Cyclone engines, was slower than the Britannia and although it had other limitations also, these were compensated for by its tremendous range and endurance.

To give an example, upon which I will elaborate later, a flight of over thirteen hours, when operating westbound to the United States or Canada, was not uncommon. My first crossing in this monster involved leaving Heathrow in the late evening, with a call at Manchester in order to uplift extra passengers. Then on to Prestwick in Ayrshire in order to fill our fuel tanks to the brim, prior to the long ocean crossing.

As happened so often in winter and indeed in spring, a huge depression sitting out in mid-Atlantic meant that at lower altitudes the wind direction was right on our nose, so much so that we would never have made the through trip, even with our maximum fuel load.

We had no option but to plan for a northerly route to Greenland and thence on down to the North American mainland. This route would take us around the top side of the depression where, as any avid television weather watcher will know, the wind flow would theoretically then be behind us. We were sure that even if this were not so, at least it would not be 'on our nose'.

124

The second problem arose from an aircraft performance factor. Although the DC-7C had powerful engines, the overall initial aircraft weight, with full passenger and fuel load, meant that it was not possible to climb to the optimum height in the early stages of a long flight.

From a navigator's point of view this meant aggravation. Initially, and it happened on this flight, the first few hours would be flown at a height of less than 10,000 feet, thereby restricting the range at which radio facilities could be received, ruling out also any chance of astronomical observations, and giving a bumpy ride through the masses of cloud associated with the weather depression. Added to this, in winter, there was the ever-present problem of ice accretion on wings, fuselage and engines.

This aircraft had the normal radio compass facility, whereby a bearing to or from a ground transmitter could be displayed. It also had equipment enabling us to use the Consol system which I have already described, together with a Loran receiver.

Fortunately, Loran stations were sited in Northern Europe, Iceland, Greenland and North America, so the further north our track took us the better the prospects of good radio reception.

Another feature, peculiar to the DC-7C, was an on-board teleprinter. Radio officers, using wireless telegraphy, had long since left the scene, and long-range radio telephony had its weaknesses, particularly in mid-Atlantic, where radio interference often resulted in garbled speech from the ground transmitter, not very helpful when one was anxiously seeking weather reports from destination and alternative airfields.

The teleprinter also had limitations, but always came up trumps once one had passed the mid-Atlantic point either way. There were two ground based transmitters, one in Newfoundland and one in Ayrshire, and the service was automatic. All one had to do was to switch on the teleprinter receiver and, range permitting, sit back while coded weather messages were hammered out at a very rapid rate.

I recall our departure from Prestwick in rain, followed by some hasty radio tuning work in order to obtain a position fix and thereby check our initial progress before radio reception deteriorated. It so happened that unforecast head winds prevailed in the opening stages and once this had been confirmed, the indications were that we were in for a long haul.

I tried the various Loran stations but although signals were

125

appearing on the cathode ray tube screen, so was interference caused by rain and static electricity, with the consequence that it needed tremendous powers of concentration and keen eyesight to sort out the radar blips from the masses of other visible interference, the 'rubbish' known as grass. However, all was not lost, since all BOAC navigation staff had been trained to apply a theoretical technique, related to air pressure and its changing values when passing through, for example, meteorological depressions.

The aircraft was fitted with a radar altimeter, which with careful tuning would give the precise true height above the sea. This height was compared with the height read off from the conventional pressure altimeter, and the difference in readings was taken to tabulations and graphs, from which one could then obtain the angle at which the aircraft was drifting off its true heading.

The theory is far too complicated to explain, but the application was easy and since the end product of drift gave us an immediate indication of our track over the surface, what more could we want?

Of course, the other aids were essential, not only as a back-up, but to cover possible human errors, yet there were many of the old hands on North Atlantic routes who would swear that they could make the complete ocean crossing relying solely on this pressure pattern flying technique, as it was called.

However bad the weather and the radio reception, there came a time when sufficient fuel had been burned off to produce a significant reduction in weight and thus permit a climb to a more favourable altitude.

This was often a worrying time, for having sat for several hours with the steady drone of four Wright Cyclones, everything suddenly came alive as the throttles were advanced to climbing power setting and the noise became deafening. It was also a time to introduce the engine superchargers, which never came into operation quietly. To explain the use of the word worrying, you must imagine yourself rumbling along in cloud, possibly with rain or ice affecting performance, when the throttles are urged forward. Probably a thousand miles from land, when a disturbing thud is heard from one engine, followed by the others, as the superchargers are brought into operation, and I could almost guarantee a jump in pulse rate. Mind you, one became accustomed to this routine after a while, and when you heard the co-pilot call 'Number 1 going in', or similar words, it was possible to prepare for the disconcerting thuds which followed and it was soon all over as the engine revolutions were gently reduced

126

to the appropriate power setting for cruising at the new higher altitude.

Once at optimum altitude, one had to be extremely unlucky not to find good incoming Loran signals or clear skies with the stars waiting to be used.

In those far off days, the navigator had two additional calculations to make at the flight planning stage. One was to calculate a point of no return, the other to determine a so-called critical point.

The former was normally associated with the weather at destination and the current fuel load. Allowing for a possible diversion after returning to the starting point, one had to calculate just how far the flight could proceed, yet still return to the departure aerodrome, should the weather so dictate.

The critical point was associated with possible engine trouble and taking two Atlantic bordering airfields such as, say, Shannon and Gander, a calculation was made to determine the point at which it would take the same time to go on as to go back. From that it followed that in the event of trouble, if you had passed the critical point you went on, if not, you turned back.

This leads to another interesting facility on the North Atlantic run, and that was the weather ship. These vessels, ex-Corvettes, I believe they were, were situated at well-chosen points along the most widely used routes. The critical point for the direct route across the Atlantic invariably occurred at, or about, longitude 35 degrees West, and so it is not surprising that one of the weather ships was sited at that longitude. These vessels were given alphabetical letters to identify them, using the standard phonetic code.

The poor soul moored in mid-Atlantic was designated weather ship J or Juliet, known to all and sundry as Ocean Weather Station Juliet. The crew of this ship provided a worthwhile and reliable service and, I might add, a comforting voice down below when many hundreds of miles from land.

These vessels were not moored in a strict sense but moved, within close limits, around a chosen geographical position, their precise position depending, I suspect, upon their ability to remain on station, weather conditions permitting.

Each was equipped with a radio beacon which apart from transmitting its identification call sign, also added coded letters or figures which conveyed the ship's precise position within a prepared grid printed on our navigation charts.

Meteorological balloon ascents were made at regular intervals and so each station was able to pass on information on the upper level temperatures, wind speed, and direction – most useful. They also had radar scanning equipment on board and would occasionally monitor an aircraft's progress and report when it was overhead.

With the ship's radio beacon transmitter tuned in on the aircraft radio compass, and their radar monitoring our progress, it was comforting to have a double confirmation when one was indeed passing overhead. On the odd occasion we were asked to make a short alteration of heading in order to identify us on their radar screen and there was just one rare occasion, at night, when Juliet reported that they could hear our engines overhead. I have no doubt that all of this added a little spice to someone's life down below and it was certainly a welcome break for us to have a brief chat in mid-Atlantic.

On one occasion when we were returning from New York in daylight, Juliet advised that they had us on their radar screen. We certainly had an indication on our own radio compass that he was dead ahead and then, with our own weather radar scanner tilted well down, we saw a minute blip on the screen, moving towards us. It was all eyes ahead, looking through broken cloud and into the wild sea down below and, there he was. Believe it or not, this was the only time we saw him.

It was difficult to hold him in sight as the sea was so rough, huge white caps everywhere, with what appeared to be a white wake trailing from his stern. There was no mistaking it, Juliet it was, and then the vessel passed below and astern and was gone. What a life, goodness knows what it was like to serve on those vessels and the crew surely deserved a medal apiece. Fortunately, with today's fast and high flying jets, there is no longer a need for the services of these vessels and as far as I know they have all been withdrawn. I trust that the crews have now retired to a quiet life in a sheltered backwater in the country, just as they so richly deserved.

However, to return to this particular flight, once settled down at optimum altitude on a westbound crossing, and weather permitting, navigation procedures became pretty routine with hourly astronomical fixes, supported in between times by signals from the many Loran stations. In addition, a fairly reliable radio beacon had been positioned at the southern tip of Greenland, providing an ideal check on progress towards the New World. My log-book records that on this occasion we were routed inbound via Goose, the airport built close by the Hamilton River inlet, in Labrador, and thence across the vast lakes and forests of North-Eastern Canada, down to join the busy airway route on into New York.

The flight time on this particular day was 12 hours and 15 minutes, and, believe me, after that length of time in the air in a noisy piston engined aircraft one felt decidedly jaded.

Conscious of the work load, before legislation took over and restricted airborne duty times, the company arranged for two bunks to be fitted at the rear of the flight deck, with an agreed occupancy time for each crew member.

It was usual for the navigator to hop in to one of the bunks, once the flight had been cleared onto an airway, but sleep was not always guaranteed, partly due to engine noise and vibration, but quite often because the pilots needed supplementary items of information including revised estimates of arrival times or fuel at destinations, if the weather showed signs of varying from that anticipated. As a consequence, even a short nap was often interrupted, without apology. Sleep whether in the air when possible, or on the ground between flights, had always been a problem, indeed in recent years it has led to official studies of jet lag and its effects.

In the 50s, the outcome was often sheer exhaustion to the extent that wind down came only after something had been provided to induce rest. That something came not in tablet form but rather out of a bottle or pump and was our good friend the glass or two of beer.

I think most crew members, if they were honest, would admit that after a long ocean crossing in bad weather, followed by around three hours on a busy airway network, the nervous system had been brought to a peak. This applied particularly when after some thirteen plus hours of flying, the crew were faced with bad weather and air traffic congestion at destination, and circumstances demanded top performance at a time when body and brain would have preferred a shut-down. In this day and age, there are legal maxima for crew duty times but since the aircraft are much faster it is still possible to operate long distance sectors efficiently and economically.

Not infrequently, I would arrive in the hotel in New York and following a couple of beers, retire to my room, switch on the television and hop into bed. Sleep seemed difficult to achieve at first, but tended to take over almost without warning. Unfortunately, with the time change between London and New York being around five hours, I often awoke, seemingly rested, to find that it was still only mid-evening. There was no alternative but to bathe, dress and walk out to see what the big city had to offer.

Even then, it was almost certain that, on return to the hotel, sleep would be difficult to achieve until the early hours, which invariably meant that part of the following day was lost. It really was a problem and it was many years before the medical experts gave proper attention to finding a solution.

In many ways, the problem was far worse if travelling eastbound. It was possible to leave London in the late afternoon and with the time change now leading to an increase in clock hours, one would arrive in the late evening by London time, which was acceptable as far as retiring to bed was concerned. However, the local time could well be say 3 am, and so having just drifted into a well-earned sleep, one would soon be awakened by all the noise of early risers and workers, who had no interest in your time change problems but solely in going about their business.

I saw this problem summed up very succinctly in a hotel 'comments' book in a Karachi hotel, close by the railway station, where one crew member had written, 'I regret to say that the 2.15 am express to Rawalpindi was 3 minutes late this morning'.

We had some very understanding medical men in BOAC and having just mentioned Karachi, I should add that one of our doctors worked long and hard until he succeeded in having the price of beer at this stopover reduced to an affordable level, thus guaranteeing those who found it beneficial, a chance to wind down and sleep without resorting to sleeping pills or the like.

For a period of around six months I journeyed to and from Canada and the United States and grew to enjoy these long hauls, once a firm in-flight navigational routine had been learned, hence I soon adjusted to a life which meant that as one left the ground at London one realised that they were confined to a small area on the flight deck for at least a half day or longer.

On one occasion, the weather situation was such that whichever route we considered, it seemed that the flight time would allow for little or no fuel reserves at our destination, Montreal. After much discussion and with characteristic determination not to let the Company down, we concluded that the only reasonable route would be well to the south where winds were lighter. So, believe it or not, I sat down and recalculated our route and fuel via the Azores. My log-book shows that it took us almost six hours to reach the Azores and then after a short refuelling stop, almost nine hours on to Montreal.

Fifteen hours flying is not a bad night's work in anybody's book. Shortly after this epic flight, I recorded the longest single flight which I have ever experienced.

With strong headwinds again forecast for the ocean crossing to Montreal, we found that there was no preferential route on that occasion and whichever way we decided to go, it would take an awful long time. We therefore chose to fly to Shannon, where we could load up with maximum fuel and take the Great Circle, or shortest route. This was fine, if one ignored the take-off run at Shannon which on this occasion seemed to go on for ever, followed by a long slow heavily laden climb, up to around 7,000 feet for the first few hours. Needless to say, this was to be another of those flights spent bouncing up and down in cloud, until we were finally able to reduce weight and climb above the weather.

It was indeed a tiring flight, with progress, as marked on my plotting chart, so slow that position fixes were little or no visible distance apart. Anyway, as always, we all settled down to our respective tasks and after the mid-Atlantic point, the first two customers crawled into the bunks.

We were routed in via Gander, in Newfoundland, and their powerful radio beacon signal, coupled with the outline of the coast ahead, on our radar screen, meant that any time at all I could take my turn in the cot and endeavour to achieve a little sleep. Sure enough, the change over took place, but no sooner had I placed my head on the pillow than I heard a sickening thud from one of the engines. Technical details do not matter, there was much activity 'up front' as the faulty engine was shut down, with rapid radio calls to the airway controller to inform him of our plight.

The DC-7C could fly quite comfortably on three engines but, of course, at much reduced speed and changed fuel consumption. We had been very tight on fuel at the outset, hence accurate time and fuel calculations for our destination now became very important. No sleep for me after all, and although I had no need to provide navigational information, since we were flying on a controlled airway, I had to keep a constant check on progress and to produce time and fuel figures, for numerous alternative airfields in case we were forced to make a diversion due to fuel shortage. In the event, we crawled our way on and into Montreal, but from Shannon, note not from London, it took us almost fourteen and a half hours and we surely earned our salaries that night.

131

CHAPTER 12

THE BIG JETS AT LAST

For some months we had watched the coming and going of the huge Boeing 707 four-engined jets, now in BOAC livery, and marvelled at their size and performance.

By today's standards I suppose that they are minnows, but 30 years ago they were giants. Like all new aeroplanes they had their teething troubles, and we heard vague stories of aircraft which had shed engines in flight, or had suffered runaway control problems involving the aircraft automatic systems, but since we were not directly involved, the tendency was to note what was happening and shed a crocodile tear or two for the crews who were engaged in the proving flights.

It was a shock for me therefore when, four days after returning from a DC-7C flight to New York, I was informed that I must operate a Boeing 707 service to Boston two days later. Perhaps it would be as well to explain that in the preceding weeks, several navigators had been called in to the Training Unit, in between flights, in order that they could be suitably briefed on the operating techniques associated with our new jet, which in any event we should all have to fly in due course. I did not realise it at that time, but I was about to enter the concluding phase of my career with BOAC, which would also be one of the most enjoyable.

Enjoyable, not so much for the routes which I subsequently flew, for I had seen it all before, but because the 707 proved to be a fast, comfortable all-weather aeroplane. It had many virtues and few vices, and my first shock when we departed for Boston in mid-November 1960, was the take-off performance. The pre-flight calculations were far more involved than for, say, a DC-7C, but provided one could obtain and maintain a high altitude slot from the air traffic control people, where the pure jet gave its most economical performance, then all was well.

Many factors had to be taken into consideration in determining the maximum take-off weight allowable, but with the huge runway length available at Heathrow these factors were seldom limiting. It was a different story at high altitude and high surface temperature airfields, where it sometimes became necessary to make last minute checks on approaching the start-of-take-off point, in case changed circumstances indicated that the aircraft was then over the maximum weight for ambient conditions.

Anyway, on this my first jet flight, the acceleration, after a slow rumbling start, pushed everyone back into their seats and it was so exhilarating as the speed built up to that required for the actual lift off, or rotation speed as it was known.

The aeroplane was 'cleaned up' immediately after take-off and as the wheels locked up and the wheel bay doors closed with a resounding thump up went the nose, and subject to appropriate clearance, we headed heavenwards like a rocket or so it seemed.

Having been accustomed to a slow laborious climb away in a heavily-laden piston-engined aircraft, a jet take-off provided quite a shock, particularly when as one passed over the airfield boundary the ground features were rapidly diminishing in size.

There came a time, following complaints from local citizens, when take-off procedures had to be modified, leading to an early power reduction after take-off, until clear of noise sensitive areas.

Gone were the noisy, slow climbs to around 7,000 feet for an hour or two. Now it was up into the wide blue yonder, and you were out of luck if early clearance was not granted to power your way up to a minimum of say 35,000 feet. On most occasions this put the aeroplane above all weather, certainly as far as cloud was concerned, and it also guaranteed excellent reception conditions for such radio aids as were then available.

One new problem now appeared on the scene however, and that was clear air turbulence and its effect on the aircraft. Doubtless readers have listened to our TV weather forecasters referring, from time to time, to the jetstreams which prevail at high levels, above depressions and associated weather fronts. Well, linked to these circumstances was the phenomenon of clear air turbulence. Because of the circumstances which led to its creation, it was possible to deduce from any rapid changes in temperature at altitude the likely occurrence of such turbulence and to do so with reasonable accuracy.

The end product was often referred to as the cobblestone effect, because the aeroplane, when subjected to this type of turbulence, felt as though it was running over cobblestones, but with violent

133

spasms injected from time to time. Unlike flying in cloud, where the type of cloud enabled one to judge the likelihood and degree of turbulence, clear air turbulence, as its name implies, could not be anticipated, unless forecast, or where an on-board expert was able to spot drastic changes in temperature which gave the all important initial clue.

The wing of the 707 was designed to flex and you may rest assured that in clear air turbulence it did just that, often to a frightening degree, although speed could be reduced to a pre-determined value in order to minimise the effect of the turbulence and thus ensure safety.

In-flight navigation routine was basically as in all previous types of aircraft, except that the equipment in the 707 had been updated and was certainly more reliable and accurate.

It still became necessary to follow more northerly tracks on occasions, for even at our new found heights, headwinds could create a major problem, particularly when, up aloft, they could exceed 200 miles per hour.

About this time, route and destination changes were taking place and our aeroplanes were now required to make what were almost trans-Polar flights. This introduced a further problem and led to a significant change in navigation procedures.

As most people know, the north magnetic pole, which determines the direction in which a magnetic compass needle will point, is not coincident with the north geographical pole and hence certain adjustments have to be made. This in itself is no problem and the compensating steering techniques have been known for ages. However, in and around the north magnetic pole the compass behaviour becomes very erratic and unreliable and finally useless. Taken to the extreme, if you were flying over the magnetic pole, a freely suspended compass needle would point downwards and a fat lot of use that would be.

So, a technique, practised by aviation experts for many years, came into general use and heading information was derived from extremely accurate gyroscopes, theoretically set, and maintained pointing to a fixed point in space, so that all headings could be steered by reference to this datum.

Charts, of course, had to be modified to cope with this change and although it is too involved to explain in a narrative of this type, suffice it to say that once learned and practised, the technique worked superbly, to the extent that even where circumstances did not dictate its use, most of us continued to use it anyway.

Ominously for the professional navigator, a new piece of equipment now appeared on the scene and as far as navigators were concerned, it threw all our past efforts and working practices aside by providing a cast-iron substitute, which did not require food, board and a salary and once the initial high cost had been written off, it became more than cost effective. It was indeed the beginning of the end for the full-time navigator and this new evil beast in a little black box was known as INS, the Inertial Navigation System. Briefly, it used the property of inertia to detect movement. Three highly sensitive gyro stabilised accelerometers were placed so that any vertical movement and movement in north/south or east/west directions, could be accurately detected. The lateral movements could, by using long established spherical trigonometrical formulae, be translated into changes of latitude and longitude.

The system was computer based and at any time, on a keyed request, could display time, distance, speed, and almost the pilot's birthday. Furthermore, with three such boxes on board, each nasty little creature could cross check its partners and correct or warn of errors as necessary. Anyway, this was for the future but it was obviously coming at us fast and for my part, with alarm bells ringing, I started to direct employment enquiries elsewhere in the aviation field, mainly to the regulatory body which, although it has changed its title many times over the years, to finally become CAA, was then MoA, the Ministry of Aviation.

In the run up to eventual resignation, or retirement as it really was, my flying was concentrated on the 707, but occasional calls for assistance from the Training Unit meant a short return to flying some of the older aircraft types, each time with a well-advanced trainee.

So, to round off this story, I will pull out a few of the flights which produced something out of routine and which, with the assistance of my flying log-book, I am able to recall as a consequence.

The Company had recently extended their American West Coast service on to Honolulu, with the object of eventually linking up with their east-bound services to Tokyo and thus provide a complete round-the-world service. In fact this plan did materialise, but en route delays, which could be tolerated by short-stage passengers, were unacceptable to travellers waiting say in Honolulu to travel on to Tokyo. Such travellers tended to opt for 'local' airlines which could provide a standby aeroplane in the event of problems. So the globe encircling schedules did not survive for long.

To the delight of flight crews, BOAC decided to position 'slip crews' in Honolulu which meant that a stopover on the beautiful island of Oahu was guaranteed. In fact, for a short while, the Company actually based some crews in Honolulu. Oh!, the agony of it all.

Anyway, to my delight, I found that in mid-December of 1960, I was rostered to operate a 707 service to Honolulu, with three-day slip crew breaks at New York and San Francisco on the way.

New York in December can be cold to say the least but it was a little too early for the heavy snows and so I was able to occupy my time with my usual walkabout outings and to concentrate on Christmas shopping.

The flight on to San Francisco was sheer pleasure for me. It consisted of controlled flying along the American airways system all the way and the work rested entirely with the pilots. I was really a dead weight, just being carried on in order to operate on the long sea crossing from San Francisco to Honolulu. For this reason, I was able to sit comfortably at my station and using the very detailed maps supplied, follow our progress across this vast continent. Initially, we headed off over Northern Pennsylvania and up to Lake Erie, thence across to the windy city.

At this time of year, the great city of Chicago, for no reason that I can explain simply looked cold, sitting at the far end of Lake Michigan, with, judging from the state of the water down below, a howling northerly wind blowing directly down from Canada and the Arctic.

This was followed by a gentle cruise across the Great Plains which were so unbelievably vast, and I sat intrigued watching every small feature as it passed below.

I was truly fascinated since I had never flown this route before, and had no vision of what to expect. Towns and cities, which I recalled mainly from American films, came and went, until finally the great mass of the Rockies, with their associated cloud could be seen in the far distance.

The ground below was now snow covered, but ahead lay a great black pool set in the snow. It was in fact the city of Denver sitting in the foothills of the Rockies.

Off to the north the towns of Cheyenne and Laramie, proof that they really did exist and were not just names thrown up by John Wayne and his kind in the Western films.

I had a long-held impression that the Rockies bordered the west coast, rather as the Andes do in South America, but here we were, only just over half way across the States and this huge mountain range already loomed ahead.

As far as the eye could see, it was nothing but brown, black, grey and even yellow mounds and peaks, which for me were so impressive that they almost defy description. It is not very often that crew members have the time, or even the inclination, to take in all that is passing below, but on this occasion I was able to make a feast of it. I could trace small rivers feeding down from the mountains, sometimes into open landscape and at other times through deep gorges. At one point I picked out a small river, which grew in size as we crossed and recrossed its path, and I noticed that it flowed through a small town with the intriguing name of Rifle. Shades of the old Wild West. I wonder how it inherited its name and if it was once a town of saloons, livery stables and even its own Boot Hill.

Following the line of this river to the south-west, I realised that in fact it was the great Colorado and the reason for its seemingly diminutive size was because the flow further upstream was being held back by the massive Boulder Dam, to the north-east.

For some time thereafter the scenery was unchanging, endless lines of jagged or rounded peaks, some slopes seemingly pine covered, almost complete wilderness and then, quite suddenly, a modern highway heading westwards would appear. Eventually to the north-west, and through a deep haze, I could just make out the Great Salt Lake and Salt Lake City. I know that film makers did their best to romanticise the great treks westward to California, but when one sees the nature of the land from the air, I think that those early pioneers deserve the credit heaped upon them by Hollywood and from that time onwards, I became far less cynical at the portrayals of their efforts.

After the Nevada Desert, there remained the short crossing of the Sierra Nevada range and then the slow descent down across the Sacramento Valley, with rapidly changing scenery, taking on a green hue, as we made the final run towards San Francisco.

If I had to choose the hotel myself, I am sure I could have done no better than my employers, who placed the crew in a first class hotel in Union Square, set in the heart of the city.

It being my first visit I had to do all the usual tourist 'things'. A fish meal at Fisherman's Wharf, a ride there and back by cable car, a tour of Chinatown, a stroll along Market Street, this being long

137

before it gained its present day reputation as a gathering point for certain groups. Finally, in the evening, a trip to 'The Top of the Mark', the Mark Hopkins Hotel, with unrestricted views over that wonderful city.

Alcatraz, the Japanese Gardens and other sights would have to wait until a later day, but fortunately I was able to contact an old RAF colleague, who was then employed by 'Flying Tigers', the locally based freight airline and with his car and his local knowledge I was transported further afield, across the mighty Bay Bridge and into Sequoia country.

There is no doubt that, under other circumstances, such a tour would have proved a costly business, but here, thanks to the necessary operational positioning of flight crews en route, it was all available, as the Americans say, practically for free.

The song says 'I Lost my Heart in San Francisco': certainly I lost mine to that wonderful city. Anyway, this story is not meant to be a tourist guide, so I will move on.

A day or so later, we were on our way again, once more along a new route but this time there would be nothing but water once we left San Francisco, until we reached the Hawaiian Islands.

As the Americans had been flying this route for many years, it had good Loran coverage, although, because the transmitters were land-based, it was not until well out from the coast, and able to pick up transmissions from stations positioned much further north, that this aid became useful.

Never mind, it was a night sector and with good weather en route, out came the sextant, and I was once more at war with the heavens. An hour or so out of San Francisco we were in high frequency radio telephony contact with Honolulu and were heartened to hear a very cheery American voice advise that the weather was CAVU, a term used to indicate ceiling and visibility unlimited. This term has now been replaced by CAVOK, loosely interpreted as ceiling (or cloud) and visibility OK. So we plodded on through the night, with astronomical position fixes every 45 minutes, until the pale glow of morning twilight, already brightening the sky behind, began to spread overhead and on towards the western horizon.

Dawn broke, to reveal a bank of cloud ahead and to our left, giving me my first sight of the line of the Hawaiian islands, nestling below the residual cloud which had built up on the previous day. Hawaii, the big island was way off to the south-west and barely visible, but the very powerful radio beacon on Oahu indicated that it lay dead ahead. As we approached what, until then, had appeared as a dark mass, one could now see the rich green vegetation along the rugged north shore and cleared inbound by our American ground controller, we slowly descended to pass between Oahu and the old leper colony island of Molokai. A gentle turn to the right and there ahead, just as if in a travel brochure, I could see the easily recognisable shape of Diamond Head, the long sandy beach of Waikiki and further ahead the vast stretch of enclosed water marking Pearl Harbor. Even at this early hour there was plenty of aircraft traffic around, but with typical American efficiency we were slotted in and were soon down on the ground.

A very rapid Customs check and then into the largest limousine I had yet seen, including those in New York. It was a stretched Cadillac and took our full crew complement of eleven souls in air conditioned comfort down to an extremely modern and comfortable hotel, just off Waikiki beach.

The next couple of days left me completely stunned, as the island took over, and long before our scheduled departure time, I wholly appreciated just why people return time and time again, such is the fascination and beauty of the islands and their people, and I am not referring to the much publicised tourist attractions.

After a few hours rest, I made my first solo sortie along the beach road and immediately picked up the lingering perfume of the ginger blossom. Apart from times when I found my way into the city of Honolulu, I don't think I lost trace of that perfume for more than a moment.

The done thing in order to really appreciate the beauty of Oahu was to hire a jeep and tour the island and this was quickly put in hand by a small group of us the next day.

Armed with a picnic lunch we set off on the long climb up and across the hilly spine of the island and then down to the rugged and rocky north shore. What a pleasure to find adequate and free parking space together with colourful well-equipped picnic sites set out along the shore at regular intervals.

Tables, bench seats, raffia sunshades, all set up ready and waiting to be used and all spotlessly clean. No damage visible anywhere so that I truly wondered if the word vandal had ever appeared in the local vocabulary.

The north side of the island is bordered by steep hills, tree or shrub lined in rich green colours almost like the jungles of Asia. We did venture up into this forest area in order to view one of the many wonderful waterfalls, a sight we were glad that we had not missed. We made a stop at the famous Sunset beach and watched fascinated as surfers negotiated breakers which must have approached double figures in height, feet of course. The temperature and humidity were reasonably high but bearably so and once moving along in the jeep, which incidentally had a fringed canopy on top, it was comfortable and relaxing. After our break, we drove on to the north and then back over the hills to run down to the opposite shore via the famous Schofield Barracks, which figured largely in the first stages of the attack on Pearl Harbor. A must, whilst driving through the pineapple fields, scattered along the road, owned by famous market names such as Dole and Del Monte, was to stop at one of the wayside huts where, for a few pennies, fresh pineapple could be sliced and eaten on the spot, most refreshing. We had a wonderful view of the huge marine base on the run down towards Honolulu, but delayed a visit to the harbour until the next day.

One attractive feature of Honolulu was the attention paid to entertaining tourists, without money being the prime consideration. For example, once a week, the Kodak Company put on a full programme of Hawaiian, Samoan and Tahitian dancing in a large open arena – indeed this show is a recognised part of any visit. True, they sold roll upon roll of their film, as visitors snapped away with their cameras and exhausted their own stock, but why not, the whole show is free anyway.

Each evening, in the International market, a beautiful shrub-lined area, just back from the beach, there was a programme, preceded by a costumed procession, of one sort of Polynesian dancing or another.

The whole atmosphere was captivating, sitting in the warm evening air, the almost overpowering scent of tropical flowers with illumination provided by huge flickering torches, attached to the trees. No pressure to see or buy, but just an invitation to sit back and enjoy the sights, sounds and perfumes of the islands.

Still behaving as typical tourists, the same group of us first paid a visit, on the next day, to the famed Aloha Tower at the dockside, scene of many a movie farewell, but I can't say that I was over impressed, although the melodious notes from the bells in the clock tower proved fascinating.

We moved on, having booked in advance, for our visit to Pearl Harbor. Knowing that we were about to visit a memorial, we had made certain that we were suitably clad as a mark of respect and in spite of the warmth, we were all wearing ties.

We were astounded therefore, when boarding the launch for the trip out, to find our fellow passengers, mostly Americans, dressed as if for a picnic with brightly coloured shirts and shorts. I must say, in fairness, that this simply gave guidance to their way of life and they obviously intended no disrespect for the occasion, as we saw when we arrived at the memorial.

Only the Americans can set things up in the manner in which the *Arizona* memorial has been established, and however one viewed the observation area and nearby chapel, the message came home fully, when one gazed down into the depths and the still visible hulk of that great battleship. I do not recall how many sailors remain entombed there, but one could do no more than stand in stunned silence, gazing down and striving to imagine what it must have been like on that day of infamy.

The visit certainly had a sobering influence and my memory of the visit remains as clear today, as then.

On our third and final day during this stopover, I wandered alone along the beach, taking in the local colour, and it far outweighed Copacabana, the Costas and anywhere else in the world for that matter.

Hearing drums and other weird instrumental noises, I headed for the local park, just inshore, where, so like the Hawaiians, there was an open air celebration in progress. As far as I could gather, it was an anniversary linked to the American occupation, if that is the correct interpretation, of Samoa. The dancing and ceremony went on for hours and was more colourful than I can describe.

Such is life on the islands, and although everyone must have their daily problems to meet and surmount, I was left with the impression that, whatever else, to be happy is the main consideration. Unfortunately, although behaving like a tourist thus far, I was still a working lad, and could not shoot off as does the true tourist to visit the other islands, all merely a short hop with the local airline.

So, all good things must come to an end, and adorned with a scented *lei*, with the compliments of the hotel, and a last *Aloha*, it was back into the air conditioned icebox of a limousine, off to the airport, reality, and the long flight home. I made several subsequent visits to the islands, but the stopovers were never boring, as there was always something new to do and see, to add to the already happy memories.

With prevailing winds from a westerly direction, the flight times homebound were very short, hence we only stopped to refuel at San Francisco and then were on our way to New York where we handed over the aeroplane to a waiting crew, while we had a two-day stopover in the Big Apple.

Being mid-December one could not have had a bigger temperature contrast than that between the gentle warm breezes of Oahu and the freezing arctic blast whistling down across the eastern seaboard, but that's travel for you.

I arrived home on the 19th of December and so the normal stand down between successive flights took me well over the Christmas period, although the much improved flight crew rostering system already had me detailed for a flight to Montreal, returning in time to provide a short break at home over the New Year festivities. Lucky me, although it was not always so.

During the month of January, life became almost commuter style since I made three flights to New York, via Boston, all pretty rapid, with little stopover time. Not that this was terribly important, since the north-east coast of America can be so cold at that time of the year, to say the least.

A change of scenery in February with Baltimore as the destination provided me with an opportunity to visit the impressive city of Washington. There is no point in cataloguing the many wonderful sights which the capital has to offer and I think that I covered most of them. I wonder if, like me, other visitors to Washington retain one memory in particular, namely that of the Marines Memorial in Arlington Cemetery. I had read of this masterpiece, and seen many photographs, but it has to be seen to appreciate its full impact. Memorials are hardly pleasant sights, but the size and form of this one in particular achieves what I take to be one of its objectives, namely that one should never forget the sacrifices made in retaking Iwojima and the many other Pacific islands. That it does for certain.

On our return to New York we were unexpectedly sent south again, to Jamaica, in order to uplift a charter group who were heading for a new life in the UK.

142

It would not be for me to pass judgement on the motives of these West Indian groups who headed for our shores, but we could hardly conceal smiles when they boarded in flimsy dresses and Ascot style hats, smart light suits, all in the warmth of Kingston, only to be almost blasted away by cold northerly winds as they descended the aircraft steps at Heathrow.

Flying in the next few years tapered off very slowly for me, as once again the basic training programme demanded that certain navigation specialists returned to the Central Training Unit, which by now was well-established in a purpose-built centre on the east side of Heathrow Airport.

As the programme peaked, we received trainees from a whole variety of sources, which again included ex-RAF pilots. As always, there was great resentment on their part at having to meet company requirements to hold a flight navigator's licence and to use it as part of the indoctrination programme.

Unfortunately, this understandable attitude presented us with problems and, as a consequence, it sometimes took a while for the training programmes to gear up. However air crew are a stoical bunch and faced with the inevitable, they generally knuckled under and came up trumps.

I think that the odd dismissal for failure to achieve the necessary standards also helped things along, after all, whatever the immediate future for these people, the long term prospects were exceedingly good.

I am quite sure that today's Jumbo and Concorde captains who suffered under this scheme, would testify to the truth of that statement, even to the value of the course.

Since successful trainees were eventually posted to a variety of routes and aircraft types, my supervisory flying had to slot in with this requirement.

So it was, that one early flight was to South Africa on the larger and latest version of the Britannia, the so called B312.

This flight proved very eventful and demonstrated how man does not always dearly love his brother. If I recall correctly, some sort of technical staff strike took place at our Heathrow engineering base, grounding pretty well all types of aeroplane. Those which were en route were allowed to complete their schedule, but crews who were positioned at 'slip' stations were simply left stranded.

There wasn't much that the company could do about that and if you were fortunate enough to be at a decent spot then it was virtually a paid overseas holiday.

We were particularly concerned on this occasion since our schedule had us arriving back in the UK just before Christmas, and now there was no indication of when aircraft were likely to leap into the air again.

Fortunately for us, or so we thought, the company had given thought to our anticipated return date and rearranged crew patterns so that when services restarted we should arrive home on Christmas Eve. This plan necessitated us transitting Rome on the way up from Cairo, rather than disembarking to hand over to another crew, as was usual.

With a song in our hearts, we landed at Rome, busily discussing the purchases which we planned to make at the airport shop during our short refuelling stop.

As the engines slowly shut down and the passenger steps were trundled out, we observed a mass of uniformed air crew moving our way, armed with briefcases and quite obviously arguing and gesticulating furiously to each other.

Passengers away, and before we could leave the flight deck, two very irate captains stepped in, each insisting that they and their crew were there to take the aircraft on to London and Christmas at home.

Our skipper floored them with the news that special provisions had been made for us to do precisely that, provisions already confirmed by a signal from London. All of this was of no avail, tempers rose, and the whole thing became terribly embarrassing so that, by mutual agreement, we all adjourned to the Station Manager's office, where the battle recommenced. From that point on, we listened to a whole gamut of excuses and reasons for stealing our aeroplane, ranging, so it seemed, from pregnancies at home, granny's funeral, measles, appointments, in fact everything but the truth, which was simply a wish to be home for Christmas. Such was the atmosphere that, in spite of right being on our side, we began to feel almost guilty, when our Captain, a gentleman if ever there was one, pointed out that the aircraft had to depart very shortly, whoever flew it to London.

A last ditch attempt was made to contact the London office by telephone, but as so often happens at such times, there was no one available with the authority needed to resolve this problem.

144

Very reluctantly, our skipper suggested, in spite of all that had been arranged, that we should hand over and allow the two remaining crews to draw lots, toss a coin, or resort to open combat if necessary, to decide who would take over.

Our very miserable group then departed for the Eternal City, where we were now condemned to spend Christmas Eve and Day at the Quirinale Hotel. Fortunately, arrangements had been made to contact our families with the bad news, and sad though it was, that was one less worry.

Every cloud, they say, has a silver lining and our's came with the superb treatment accorded to us at the hotel over the festive season. There were many airline crews accommodated at this hotel and the management laid on a first-class meal supplemented by a good supply of appropriate beverages all in a large lounge which had been set aside for us.

I can still hear the words of our Captain after the Christmas meal, when somewhat haughtily and slightly inebriated he rose to address the assembled throng as things began to warm up. 'Ladies and gentlemen (there were many stewardesses present), as the senior Captain, of the senior airline present' – that was as far as he got when a huge Australian Qantas airline Captain hurled back 'Yea, but you can't play flaming cricket'.

That really set the mood for the evening and if one had to spend Christmas away from home, you could not have wished for a better atmosphere or group of companions. We did in fact fly home on Boxing Day, but by that time the drama was behind us and it was just another ride home.

Shortly after, I was hauled out at short notice, together with a trainee, to operate a DC-7F service from Manchester to Montreal. The 7F was a freighter version of the aircraft which I had previously flown to the New World, so in a navigational sense nothing was new. The load however was, for amongst the usual wide variety of crates and containers was one huge wooden box with large canvas slings attached. In these slings, believe it or not, were porpoises. I cannot remember precisely how these poor creatures were stowed, but apart from a need for their handler to keep them moist, he had also to constantly smear their skins with what I was told was lanolin. My student and I were far too busy to take any interest in the welfare of the porpoises during the ocean crossing, but watching the procedure as they were unloaded at Montreal, I felt nothing but pity for these creatures, who if they are as intelligent as we are told, must have taken a poor view of the human race. I don't know where their ultimate destination was but one could only hope that they survived to forget that cold and noisy journey by air. An afterthought was that had we force landed in the sea, for any reason, the porpoises would have had the last laugh.

Life continued at a hectic pace, one moment expounding deep theory in a classroom, then into the air once more to see theory put into practice.

By 1963, signals were coming through loud and clear, that like it or not, navigators, as such, were on the way out, the work in future to be covered by pilots who were already well trained anyway, coupled with more sophisticated on-board navigational equipment.

In the inevitable run down period, I had one more opportunity to undertake a long-range flight, when I was rostered out to San Francisco via New York. Nothing new about that, but on arrival at destination, I was bundled on to a United Airlines flight and down to Los Angeles, where I was to operate one of the first direct flights from there to London.

It goes without saying that I made the most of my one and only visit to that city, where crews were accommodated in a cosy residence at Santa Monica beach. Hollywood was a must and I did it all including standing at the corner of Hollywood and Vine, Groumans Chinese Theater and of course the Grand Drive along Wilshire Boulevard.

The flight home was not over long, thanks to a strong prevailing westerly wind most of the way but the track was much further north than I had flown before. It took us up over Winnipeg, Hudson Bay, Northern Labrador and mid-Greenland thence down to Prestwick and on into London. From Hudson Bay onwards I saw some of the most inhospitable territory ever, and blessed Rolls-Royce for the four engines which were powering our 707 safely along. In all, the flight took a little over ten hours, a long time for a 707, but a short time for the distance travelled. It was on this flight that I saw a strange phenomenon which, in fact, took a while to sort out.

Heading for home, somewhere over the North Atlantic, we were thousands of feet above a solid mass of white cloud, which lay like an unending blanket as far as the eye could see. Looking ahead and below I could see a long black finger, or line, which seemed to come from behind and cease at a point ahead of us, just on top of the cloud. As we moved ahead, so it moved with us and I could only conclude that it was another aircraft way down below, churning along just above or in the cloud tops. However, if there were other aircraft in the vicinity one could invariably hear their radio telephony calls to the various control centres giving their present position, yet at this time no such calls could be heard.

It was quite a while before the mystery was solved when the penny dropped with a loud clang. The sun was dropping towards the western horizon and unbeknownst to us, we were streaming a large condensation trail behind the engines, a sight which ground observers must have seen many times when meteorological conditions were right.

The black line was in fact the shadow of our own condensation trail, cast on to the cloud bank below, and as we moved forward, so the shadow traced our path across the cloud.

It was, to me, quite a remarkable sight, not seen by many people, I'll warrant, but of course as the sun set in the west, and darkness crept in ahead of us so this shadow slowly disappeared, never to be seen again by me, at least.

Alarm bells were sounding everywhere now and BOAC were busy endeavouring to negotiate an acceptable deal with their navigators, whereby redundancy terms could be set up.

I immediately began to search around, sounding out prospective employers, before the inevitable exodus took place.

I wonder if the present manager of Biggin Hill Aerodrome remembers the fright which he gave me when I enquired after employment. For a pittance he said that I could help to set up the administrative organisation there, working, on average, around eighty hours per week and on call in between times. No further comment!

Fortunately for me, the aviation regulatory body, at that time the Ministry of Aviation, had set up a small group of examiners who were required to prepare, operate and mark the various theoretical examination papers, linked with professional flight crew licences.

In that group, was an old colleague who advised that whilst there were no vacancies immediately, retirements were pending, and then the hunt would be on for replacements.

His suggestion was that I should make early application for any operational post with the Ministry and then sit tight until the examiner vacancies came up.

For my part, it was a difficult decision to make, since by leaving BOAC before the general exodus, I would forego a golden handshake, the amount of which was yet to be agreed. In truth, the corporation, accepting that they wanted navigators out anyway, were very helpful and made me an offer, which whilst it fell short of the ultimate pay-off, was nonetheless generous, so I took it and departed.

CHAPTER 13

THE FINAL WIND DOWN

So it was, that late in 1964, I became one of a group of ex-air crew members, who were known as Operations Officers and were now full-time civil servants.

The appointment as Operations Officers had been in existence for many years and the duties covered a wide range of interests, all obviously with a direct connection to flying.

My first task was extremely demanding and taxed my powers of persuasion and diplomacy to the limit. Aircraft noise had become a major problem in and around Heathrow and so the Ministry, in their wisdom, arranged for the construction of a publicity caravan, equipped with a small exhibition, a cinema screen to be supported by a skilled projectionist, an air traffic expert and guess who, me!

Our task was to visit every community within a radius of about ten miles from the perimeter of Heathrow, and explain to 'Joe Public' just what the Ministry of Aviation was doing to keep noise levels to a minimum.

In fairness, they were doing their best, since noise monitoring posts were situated along the take-off flight paths, special after take-off procedures were introduced and offending airlines punished.

That was all very well, but just try explaining, that to an irate citizen who lives just off the end of the main runway, particularly when he cannot hear your explanation thanks to thundering jets passing overhead at that point in time.

Slowly I evolved a technique, and had answers to most of the awkward questions, always with a friendly reassuring smile, of course.

Our worst critics fell into two groups. The first were mainly characters leaving the local pub after a jar or two, and who were just spoiling for a fight. I confess that I picked up one or two choice new words from time to time, but we never came to blows. I found that noting their names, with a promise of further action and advice, usually did the trick.

The second group were mums on their way home from collecting the little ones from school. They loved a good verbal battle and I'm sure that in some instances it added a little something to their otherwise routine lives. One dear soul presented me with stained babies clothing and asked me what I was going to do about it. I could not convince her that my business was to deal with aircraft noise complaints, she simply wanted to know why my bloody aeroplanes had dropped this muck on her washing.

To pacify her, I accepted the soiled linen and arranged for it to go off to a Government laboratory for analysis. I was delighted to be able to tell her, at a later date, that the offending mixture had been fired out of the rear end of an overflying bird and consisted, in part, of the undigested remains of certain small berries and had nothing to do with our 'bloody aeroplanes'.

There was a more serious side to the problem and we had to deal with a very vociferous group, the Noise Abatement Society. They handled their case complaints very efficiently and as time has shown, they obtained pretty well all that they sought by way of noise reduction and the provision of sound proofing costs where justifiable.

One interesting job did come my way, when in response to frequent complaints from Lady Zia Wherner, at Luton Hoo, I was despatched to that stately home in the hope that I could sort out her problem.

Lady Zia's concern was the noise from aircraft which had just taken off from Luton Airport, particularly at weekends when members of the Royal Family might be staying at the house. The offenders, who were pilots of minor charter companies and had a living to make, hotly contested the accusations, leaving me to resolve a situation of impasse.

The solution came, after consultation with the Royal Aircraft Research Establishment people at Farnborough, who produced a Polaroid camera, with a grid which could be superimposed over the lens. By careful use of this camera, it was possible to photograph the aircraft passing overhead and to determine their height, with reasonable accuracy. By comparing the aircraft's image against the grid, whether accurately or not, we were able to convince the aircraft operators that we could check their height and they took steps to avoid Luton Hoo thereafter.

I was quite surprised to be accorded a very warm welcome to the big house and was frequently invited to lunch, where I found that somewhat imperious lady to be a delightful hostess. Even more pleasant was the arrival, after the job had been completed of a postman bearing a brace of fat pheasants delivered to our door with the compliments of Sir Harold. They also gave me a copy of their stud book, for as most people know they were great blood stock and racing folk, but I never had occasion to apply the information for personal gain.

After about a year a public notice invited applications for the post of flight crew examiner and my request went in like a shot.

With all due modesty, if I may say so, my total experience both in teaching and operating, plus the fact that I was almost a sitting tenant, won the day for me and, after a somewhat lengthy promotion board, I was in. So the words of advice given to me by my old colleague, many months before, had proved very worthwhile.

It was a strange new life at first, for the examining team was accommodated in the heart of London and until my arrival consisted of a number of ex-merchant navy master mariners and a couple of ex-RAF navigators, who had little or no civil flying experience.

This gave me a wonderful opportunity, once I had got to grips with their procedures and standards, to introduce a very positive civil slant into examination questions. In truth, this gave tremendous interest to the work and provided me with total job satisfaction.

The holding of a current Flight Navigator's Licence was a prerequisite for the job and the Ministry agreed to provide me with the necessary flying time in order to keep my experience up to date and the licence valid. The best deal for this purpose was, oddly enough, with the Irish airline, Aer Lingus, and for a number of years I shuttled to and fro across the Atlantic on their 707 flights.

At that time, this airline employed a fair number of ex-RAF people, hence the flying routine was very much on a par with the BOAC procedures. Certainly, the aircraft and crews left nothing to be desired.

Strangely enough, it was on one of these not too frequent flights with the Irish airline, that I had one of my most disturbing experiences, after so many years in aviation.

We had departed from New York and were about an hour or so out from Gander, when we received a frantic radio telephony message from New York advising that an anonymous telephone call had been received to say that there was a bomb on board our aircraft.

It is difficult to describe our immediate reaction, for we had no idea as to how we should handle the situation. It was not possible to brief the passengers since that could have led to panic, neither could we commence a search, for the same reason, and in any event, who knew what to look for?

At times like this, there is only one realistic approach, which is to get down as soon as possible, but halfway across the North Atlantic makes that somewhat difficult, to say the least.

So the decision, since we had a strong tailwind behind us, was to carry on to Shannon or Dublin and let fate take care of the rest. What thoughts went on in other minds is anybody's guess and I wonder how many silent prayers were offered. For my part, I kept myself as busy as possible with the navigation task, lapsing occasionally to consider how the end might come. Would it be instantaneous, as a massive explosion, or would it be a minor bang, possibly followed by an explosive decompression of the fuselage or maybe a slow drift down in to the sea.

Since I am now relating the story, we obviously made it to Dublin and the whole thing was written off as a hoax, after the aeroplane had been pretty well stripped down for inspection.

Hoax it may well have been, but try sitting in an aeroplane in mid-Atlantic, with a bomb threat hanging over you, and include a hoax as one of the possible options. No further comment is necessary.

As an examining team, our word was law and the wretched candidates walked in fear of our small group of specialist monsters.

It was during this period, that several of the British professional pilot training schools began courses of training for a whole number of foreign airline students, the major input being from Iraq and Libya. Many of us believed at that time, that the number of trainee pilots was far too high for the size of these foreign national airlines, and it was suspected that more than a few of these people went home and on to fly for the military. I wonder if we were right in our thoughts?

The general expansion in training gave us an opportunity to get out and about, since the regulatory body was required to approve and inspect all professional training staff and establishments. We set up a good rapport with training staff and there is no doubt that our combined efforts led to the universally recognised high standards in the United Kingdom and the consequential inflow of foreign business.

Certain foreign students were notorious for using any trick in the book to achieve examination passes, to the extent that on one occasion I was called to deal with a case wherein a large sum of money suddenly appeared in a rolled up bundle beneath the examinee's table. When I asked him if it was his, the examinee gave me a smile which would have done credit to one of Hollywood's best, but that was all. When I repeated the question his eyes said all that his voice would undoubtedly have liked to utter. I cautioned him that unless he picked up the money he would face disqualification. It was all part of the game as he saw it but he had lost and I suppose he thought it was worth a try. When subsequently I discussed the matter with my Director, he said, with a gleeful chuckle, you should have counted the money, and if it exceeded your anticipated future salary, plus pension rights, then it was worth considering. A joke, of course – I think!

I saw my aviation career out in this field and had the good fortune, in my last few years of working life, to take over the appointment of Chief Examiner, heading this cheerful and efficient team. Unfortunately, at the same time I ran into the 'knockers' and accountants, who in many fields and without detailed knowledge of the work, came in with the object of convincing policy makers that they could provide more cost effective alternatives to the existing systems. There is always room and time for change but my last few years were spent in never-ending battles against such people.

As specialist examiners, we had always resisted slick, cheap, rapid result systems practised elsewhere in the world, and we were on record internationally as being totally opposed to these techniques. It was significant that in spite of our stance, foreign airlines still sent their students in thousands to this country where the United Kingdom licence was rated as one of the finest, being accepted at face value on a worldwide basis.

However, European Union lying ahead, and training costs rising steadily, something had to give, and the existing subjective examination system was first to go.

What exists today in that field, will always be at a lower academic standard than that which I thought to be necessary, but I am told that the gold plated product is no longer required and certainly the present one is cheaper, so I guess that is what is regarded as progress. I have always thought that the change now introduced into the assessment of standards has followed the general pattern of education today and from what I now see, that isn't saying much.

I am proud to say that when I metaphorically handed in my maps and charts and other tools of my trade, I was still fighting to retain standards and although opponents saw me as a dinosaur, I fought for what I thought to be right, I might even say, knew to be right. Anyway, regardless of what I feel or say, the aeroplanes will go on flying, keen intelligent young men will handle them efficiently and, if theoretical knowledge standards are somewhat down, perhaps it doesn't really matter, or will never be important enough to show.

I spent forty-five years in the aviation profession and would not have changed my life for worlds, and that includes my wartime flying too, and if I had my life to lead again, would I do the same? You bet I would!

In conclusion, may I say of my old 'Airways' colleagues who read this book, 'Please leave your critic's hat in the wardrobe and remember that at our age memories fade a trifle so that any minor misspelling of names and places, or the use of a little licence, must be forgiven!'

FOOTNOTE

Eric Woods was Invested with the Livery of the Guild of Air Pilots and Air Navigators in 1978, and subsequently served on the Court of that Company, as an Assistant for three years.

He holds that worthy Livery Company's Master Air Navigator Certificate and in 1983 received the Master's Certificate of Commendation for services to aviation training over a period of forty years.

INDEX